WHAT EVERY
SAINT
NEEDS TO KNOW ABOUT
LUCIFER

Judy Flanagan

DESTINY IMAGE AFRICA™

An Imprint of

DESTINY IMAGE EUROPE™ srl
Via Maiella, 1
66020 San Giovanni Teatino (Ch) - Italy

"Changing the world, one book at a time."

This book and all other Destiny Image Europe™ books are available at Christian bookstores and distributors worldwide.

To order products, or for any other correspondence, please contact:

DESTINY IMAGE EUROPE™ srl
Via Acquacorrente, 6
65123 - Pescara - Italy
Tel. +39 085 4716623 - Fax: +39 085 4716622
E-mail: info@eurodestinyimage.com

Or reach us on the Internet: **www.eurodestinyimage.com**

ISBN-13: 978-88-89127-49-0

For Worldwide Distribution, Printed in Italy.

1 2 3 4 5 6 7 8/10 09 08 07

DEDICATION

Sincere thanks to my daughter, Juliette, for all her help and encouragement and without whose support this book would never have been completed. Also to Paul and Debbie for their "techno" assistance and to Neil for his support.

I dedicate this book to all my children and their spouses with whom God has blessed me. Each one brings their unique freshness into His kingdom, and my life.

ACKNOWLEDGMENTS

My heartfelt thanks to Sandra Evangelista Ciccone at Destiny Image Europe for all her assistance and suggestions.

Also many thanks to my 88-year-old mother who helped me compose the Daily Covering Prayer on page 161. She has traveled on this warrior road with me for over 35 years; and as delicate as she is now, she can still put the devil to flight!

ENDORSEMENT

One of the keys to military victory is to *know your enemy*. As true as this statement is for the physical realm, so it is likewise for the spiritual. The Church of today needs to recognize, at this time as much as any other time in human history, the subtlety and the tactics of the enemy; but more than even these, the Church must recognize the victory that we already have over the enemy. We stand on victorious ground through the wonder of Christ and the awesome power of His blood! Judy's book has proved to be most beneficial in helping me to personally recognize these truths.

The wonder of our authority in the spiritual realm brings with it brand-new understanding of spiritual warfare. Our victory will not be won on a physical battlefield, but at the place of prayer in the spiritual realm, just as Moses prayed for victory against the Amalekites (see Exod. 17).

I trust that this book will both instruct and inspire you on to victory through the Name that is above every name!

Pastor Trevor H. Downham
Norwegian Settlers Church, Port Shepstone, South Africa

TABLE OF CONTENTS

FOREWORD

When Jesus Christ said, *"It is finished"* on the cross at Calvary, He meant that He had completed the mission for which He came to earth to accomplish. Christ, the second Adam, had legally recovered the earth and put it back once again into mankind's hands, after the first Adam had carelessly relinquished it and placed it into satan's possession.

This book explains how the triangle of Adam, satan, and the Messiah fought for dominion of the planet Earth. Christ won; He paid a dear price to legally take back the dominion of the earth and place it once again firmly into the hands of man.

It is the duty of every blood-washed, born-again believer to maintain the control of the earth and limit satanic influence in the lives of mankind. We are to hold *all the ground our Savior purchased by His death*. "… and [Jesus] said unto them, *Occupy till I come"* (Luke 19:13). And we are expected to do this with all the abilities and promptings of the Holy Spirit and use the armor given to us by God for our protection. This book tells you how to be worthy of being a soldier in Jesus Christ's army.

Often, Christ is pictured as a gentle, meek, and mild Savior; but how many Christians know that He is the Commander in Chief of the hosts of Heaven? He has called each born-again believer to train to be a soldier (see 1 Tim. 1:18; 2 Tim. 2:3-4). This book is intended to enable you to be ready, able, and willing to join Him in the last-days battle that takes place at Armageddon. "See, the Lord is coming with thousands upon thousands of His holy ones" (Jude 14b NIV).

INTRODUCTION

The supernatural is very real. Whether it be "good" or "bad," it does actually, factually exist. Mankind's interest in the unseen has gathered momentum in this era like never before.

People have been bombarded with supernatural heroes, and have become immune by the never-ending flow of violence on our televisions, computer games, and cinema screens. We have been indoctrinated by these sources to think that if someone offends you, it is okay to retaliate—even permissible to maim or kill. Death does not shock us anymore.

Morals have been distorted, and we've been indoctrinated with the idiom, "*If it feels good, I can have it or do it!* No restrictions must be placed on me. I am in charge of my own life." This thinking ultimately leaves us with no boundaries or perimeters for our conscience to speak to us.

Satanic bondage is the major concern of our generation. Lack of understanding and directions due to the banning of religious teaching in our schools have lost our children their spiritual identity. The reading material in schools includes wizards, witches, mediums, trolls, magicians, crystal balls, spells, hexes, and anything supernatural; so, we take out the religious instruction from the curriculum, but include the foregoing subjects in our reading matter! Consequently, which way are we pointing this new generation? Add dungeons and dragons, tarot cards, and the ouija board, and we discover that children have lost their moorings and morals, and need an anchor to fulfill their emotional and spiritual needs.

Unfortunately, parents either totally disbelieve in a real devil and evil spirits or swing the other way and feel an unnatural interest in them. By denying any *genuine* spiritual information in our schools (and remember, that man is made up of body, soul, *and spirit*), the body and brain are being catered for; but the "spirit" is not being fed godly concepts, so our youth go in search of it for themselves. Many seek it through the television media and films showing occult practices, because there is a spiritual void.

Music lyrics, sex, and violence are corrupting the values of our youth. Many rock stars are into some form of the occult, and it's belted out in lyrics and beat for our youth to digest. The Scriptures tell us that pipes and timbrels were created in lucifer (see Ezek. 28:13 KJV), so he has the music industry well covered. Not all music is corrupted, but all heavy metal rock is distinctly occultish.

As the world is plugging the occult and the perverse supernatural, it is a natural progression for our youth to fall for the deception of satan. And believe it or not, there is a very real devil, and there is a very real supernatural world out there. But how can parents protect themselves from evil affecting and influencing the lives of our families? In this real world, we can't send for Arnold Schwarzenegger. This is reality, so we have to learn to handle things for ourselves…and it is an ongoing battle.

Note that terrorism, crime, murder, rape, abortion, and child molestation have never been so prolific and constant. And during your lifetime, sooner or later, one or more of these horrors will touch *your life*. If you live on this planet, there is no escaping it. But what can one person do? Lie down and take all that life throws at you…or fight back!

There has always been a distinct line between good and evil, and if we are to get back to reality, we have to use "spiritual" methods to fight "spiritual" things. By delving into that antiquated book, the Bible, we look for answers, and it brings forth some interesting facts.

Every person on earth lives on a relentless battlefield with the invisible world of satan and his hordes; no one is exempt. But there is hope. The most authenticated ancient book in existence is the Bible, and digging into it sheds a most unexpected light on the world of the supernatural. Read for yourself how we coexist with the supernatural and how we can either let the world lead us by the nose or we can take our life and destiny into our own hands. But it will first require a decision and a stand to be made before we are able to do this.

The Bible speaks of a glorious army (see Joel 2:2-11)—one that can and does overcome evil! In fact, the whole last Book of the Bible—called "Revelation"—is about "overcomers." The Bible is fact, not some Hollywood fictional screen hero out to save the world. There is something each one of us can do—we can either join this "glorious army," or we can let life and other forces rule our lives.

On a fact-finding mission in the Bible, I found a caring, loving God who knows what evil plagues the lives of every being on the planet, and He gives us answers and the ability to belong to this glorious army that can withstand the trauma of living on earth today. It reveals that there are two major powers at work in the universe—the power of good, whose head is God, and the power of evil, whose head is the devil. Our first priority is to decide on whose side we want to be— God's or the devil's?

This is survival. To be a fence-sitter is to face disaster with no help. You will still come under satanic attack even if you don't want to throw your lot in with God. You don't receive exemption because you choose not to fight. Inevitably, a decision has to be made. If you are not victim material, you must be a fighter, which leaves you with only one real decision to make. You will have to attach yourself to God— find out what you can about His glorious army and train to be an overcomer of evil. Your life and family will then belong to you through God; you will not be at the whim of any evil supernatural force that wants to damage or destroy all that you hold dear.

This is war. You didn't declare it, but while you live on this planet Earth, you are automatically caught up in this ancient battle between good and evil. The Bible says if you throw in your lot with God, you'll be known by a new name—a Christian! Come with me on this trip through the Scriptures in an attempt to evolve into an *overcomer*.

Everything has a beginning or a foundation; Christianity came about by a loving God who sent His Son to reproduce Himself in man-form in the womb of the virgin Mary. Jesus had none of the advantages of being God while on earth; indeed, for God's plan of salvation to succeed, Christ had to be as human as Adam was, because God had already put the earth under Adam's dominion or authority. Adam gave away that authority by obeying satan in the garden of Eden. So, it would take a "man" to claim back the earth for mankind and put mankind back in authority—legally.

It was not a loser who hung on the cross, but a man who had been given the commission of Father God to save mankind and reconcile man unto God. How great was the love of Jesus for mankind to have laid down His life as He hung naked and shamed on Calvary's cross. That is why He was able to say with His last breath on earth…"It is finished!" He had completed the task God had sent Him to do.

Since that time, anyone who calls on the name of the Lord, accepts that Jesus carried their sins on the cross, and accepts the salvation that comes with the sacrifice that Jesus made, will be known as a "believer," "saint," or "redeemed one!" We can't begin to know who our enemy (the devil) is, and engage him in battle, until we know who we are.

1

GOD GIVES AT SALVATION

Neither is there salvation in any other: for there is none other name under heaven given among men, whereby we must be saved (Acts 4:12).

Acceptance of Jesus Christ as your Savior gives:

1. Salvation—eternal life.

2. Deliverance.

3. Healing (of the cracks and fissures of our spirit; and also for our body and mind).

4. Preservation (of spirit—not necessarily the body).

5. Forgiveness of sins.

The enormity of who you really are since you accepted Christ as your Savior has to be firmly fixed in your mind. Imagine the following.

Wave after wave of armed military might rolls past, and the president of the United States takes the salute. Countless thousands from the various branches of the infantry pass in well-drilled formation.

They are followed by endless rows of trucks and armor-plated troop carriers. Behind them follow giant tanks mounted on flatbed trailers. Row after row of rocket launchers, ground–to-air missiles, and missiles capable of both conventional and nuclear warhead fittings bring up the rear in what military observers from other parts of the world describe as being one of the most formidable displays of military hardware ever staged in the world.

Are you impressed? If I told you that every *true* believer is potentially far more dangerous than the most dangerous nuclear warhead, would you laugh at me? Yes? Consider a nuclear weapon.

1. It has to have someone give it direction.

2. It has to have a target—something tangible.

3. It can destroy continents, obliterating whole nations, killing mankind by the millions.

4. But amidst all the carnage of such an event, when men die, their spirits at death will still go to their designated destiny—either Heaven or hell.

However, consider the enormity of weaponry that:

1. Operates on its own (a Holy Spirit, empowered believer).

2. Can fight against a target it cannot see (in another realm).

3. Fights not just for the bodies, but also for the spirits of mankind.

4. Is able to destroy and remove, single-handedly, unwanted spiritual forces.

5. Can change the destiny of both the world and man's final abode.

That's power—power that all the scientists in the world are unable to harness! Each true believer has that *power*. Can you realize the potential of an army of believers if every man used this *power* to the fullest?

Wouldn't it be great to have the Lord Jesus, as our Commander in Chief, stand on the rostrum and take the salute, as the army of believers marches past showing all their might and power? None of the displays that the world puts on to impress its neighbors of its nuclear strength could ever match it. But unfortunately, the only sight the world would see is millions of believers marching past without a visible weapon in their hands...I don't think we would impress them. But *we know our strength*; this is the army that Jesus Christ is coming back for—a victorious one and a powerful one. The fact that we have eternal life should cause us to be radical! The most sophisticated weaponry that mankind can devise will never compare with it.

Now, you might be saying, "But what is this power I'm supposed to have that will enable me to fight the enemy?" In your own strength, you have none. You are no match for your arch enemy, satan, or the thousands of years of deceit and strategy of his agents. You would fall flat on your face if you tried *to fight satan in your own strength*.

But the one to whom we belong, Jesus Christ, came to this earth to do a specific mission for His Father. God loves Jesus very much; in fact, They are one. The tremendous love Father God has for Jesus Christ needs to be pointed out because it is *inconceivable* that God would send His beloved Son Jesus to earth, to fight against satan and his hordes in order to retrieve the earth again for mankind, *if He had never given Him the necessary weapons and ability to overcome them.*

When Jesus left the earth after His death and resurrection, He gave a command to His disciples—the disciples then and the ones now: "*Go ye into all the world*" (see Mark 16:15-18) and "*As My Father hath sent Me, even so send I you*" (John 20:21b).

Now, what kind of Commander would we have if Jesus sent us out to fight the enemy, but unlike Father God did for Jesus, *He forgot to give us the ability, power, and weaponry needed to combat the enemy?*

As we know from Scripture, Jesus did overcome satan on Calvary and He triumphed over him. When Jesus said, "*It is finished*," as He hung on the cross, He was referring to the task He had been given by His Father to do. His earthly job was completed! During His lifetime, Jesus fought the devil using the weaponry of obedience, righteousness, purity, love, and the Word of God.

When God looks at the saints, He doesn't see our inabilities and imperfections; He sees us through the righteousness and ability of Jesus Christ. *We are the righteousness of God in Christ Jesus.*

Jesus fought satan with righteousness; the saints are the righteousness of God in Christ Jesus. The apostle Paul said, *"Not having mine own righteousness, which is of the law, but that which is through the faith in Christ, the righteousness which is of God by faith"* (Phil. 3:9b).

And, *"But of Him are ye in Christ Jesus, who of God is made unto us wisdom, and righteousness..."* (1 Cor. 1:30). Using Christ's righteousness as our shield, the weakest and youngest of God's army *has power.*

There is one more thing I would like to share with you before we learn more about our enemy, because it shows the complete love and care the Lord Jesus has for His disciples.

THE TRUTH ABOUT THE GARDEN OF GETHSEMANE

Through the ages, the interpretation of what happened in the Garden of Gethsemane has cast a slur upon the commitment and integrity of our Messiah, Jesus Christ. The clergy have perpetuated this lie with the utmost sincerity and best intentions. But it is now time to expose the lie that Jesus, through His humanity, asked the Father to take away the cup of suffering He was about to endure because of the horrific pain of the crucifixion and also because He would have to take on the sins of mankind.

For several decades, I had formed the habit of reading my Bible daily, but whenever I came to the 26th chapter of Matthew, I would skip over it because it distressed me. However, one day, the Lord prompted me to go back over the scene in Gethsemane.

> *Then cometh Jesus with them unto a place called Gethsemane, and saith unto the disciples, Sit ye here, while I go and pray yonder. And He took with Him Peter and the two sons of Zebedee, and began to be* **sorrowful** *and very heavy. Then saith He unto them, My soul is ex-* **ceeding sorrowful***, even unto death: tarry ye here, and watch with Me. And He went a little farther, and fell on His face, and prayed, saying, O My Father, if it be possible,* **let this cup pass from Me***: nevertheless not as I will, but as Thou wilt. And He cometh unto the*

*disciples, and findeth them asleep, and saith unto Peter, What, could ye not watch with Me one hour? Watch and pray, that ye enter not into temptation: the spirit indeed is willing, but the flesh is weak. He went away again the second time, and prayed, saying, O My Father, **if this cup may not pass away from Me, except I drink it**, Thy will be done. And He came and found them asleep again: for their eyes were heavy. And He left them, and went away again, and prayed the third time, **saying the same words**. Then cometh He to His disciples, and saith unto them, Sleep on now, and take your rest: behold, **the hour** is at hand, and the Son of man is betrayed into the hands of sinners* (Matthew 26:36-45).*

These verses had always disturbed me, especially the part that Jesus had asked the Father to "*take away*" the cup He was about to endure. There seemed something cowardly in this request.

I had had the concept explained to me that *Jesus, in His humanity, did not want to face the agony of the cross, and especially did not want the sins of the world poured out upon Him, because He knew it would separate Him from the Father.*

Yet, First John 3:8b says, "*For this purpose the Son of God was manifested, that He might destroy the works of the devil.*"

This Scripture made the explanation even more difficult to accept. It didn't fit with the image I had of the Messiah. It seemingly revealed a personality change—a weak side to Jesus, and I could never accept that Jesus had a weak side. Hence, I continued to skip over any verses dealing with Gethsemane.

Let's consider the first point: "*His reluctance to be crucified*" and find out what the Scriptures say about this.

I was not rebellious, neither turned away back. I gave My back to the smiters, and My cheeks to them that plucked off the hair; I hid not My face from shame and spitting. For the Lord God will help Me; therefore shall I not be confounded: therefore have I set My face like a flint, and I know that I shall not be ashamed (Isaiah 50:5b-7).

Christ is "*the Word of God*" and, therefore, the written Word of God, as stated clearly in Isaiah in the foregoing verse, was no surprise to

Jesus. He *knew* what was ahead of Him on the cross. He *knew* what to expect even before He came to earth.

> *As many were* [astounded] *at Thee; His visage was so marred more than any man, and His form more than the sons of men* (Isaiah 52:14).

> *He is despised and rejected of men; a man of sorrows, and acquainted with grief: and we hid as it were our faces from Him; He was despised, and we esteemed Him not....But He was wounded for our transgressions, He was bruised for our iniquities: the chastisement of our peace was upon Him; and with His stripes we are healed* (Isaiah 53:3,5).

> *That it might be fulfilled which was spoken by Isaiah the prophet, saying, Himself took our infirmities, and bare our sicknesses* (Matthew 8:17).

> *But those things, which God before had shown by the mouth of all His prophets, that Christ should suffer, He hath so fulfilled* (Acts 3:18).

> *I lay down My life* [willingly] *for the sheep* (John 10:15b).

Jesus was in God's hands from the beginning to the end of His life. He had always kept Himself in the center of God's will; and it was God's will for Christ to redeem mankind in the manner He did at the crucifixion.

Jesus Christ was born to die!

And yet we are to believe that only an hour before His arrest, He had been so *unwilling to do so* that He had asked the Father three times to take the "cup" of suffering from Him, meaning *He didn't want to go to the cross*!

The second point: Regarding the "sins of the world" that Jesus was supposed to be reluctant to take upon Himself because He feared separation from God...

> *Who gave Himself for our sins, that He might deliver us from this present evil world, according to the will of God and our Father* (Galatians 1:4).

The promises of the coming Messiah in Genesis and throughout the Old Testament are precise and repetitive.

In the beginning was the Word, and the Word was with God, and the Word was God (John 1:1).

And the Word was made flesh, and dwelt among us [this was Jesus] (John 1:14a).

Hence, as the Word of God Himself, Jesus knew anything written in the Bible; He knew every word, because He is the Word, in both the Old and New Testaments. He knew all about the sacrifices and offerings required by the Father for the covering of sins.

In Leviticus chapter 16, God required the Old Testament priests to place their hands symbolically on the head of a goat, confess their personal sins over it, and send it into the wilderness. Then the priest sacrificed another goat, spilling its blood on the altar as a sacrifice. This was required to atone for the sins of Israel.

In burnt offerings and sacrifices for sin Thou hast had no pleasure. Then said I, Lo, I come (in the volume of the book it is written of Me) **to do Thy will, O God** (Hebrews 10:6-7).

An innocent animal, without blemish or defect, was sacrificed for the sins of the nation of Israel, just as an innocent Lamb (Jesus), without blemish or defect, would be sacrificed for the sins of the world. Jesus knew there was no other way of expiating the sins of the world and reconciling man unto God.

That was the absolutely only purpose of the Messiah coming to earth.

From the beginning, Jesus knew exactly what was expected of Him before He came to earth. He was to be a sacrifice for the sins of mankind, the atonement for sin, and the reconciliation between man and God. There was no other way than sacrifice, to reconcile man unto God. Jesus knew what was required of Him before He came to earth.

Then said I, Lo, I come: in the volume of the book it is written of Me, I delight to do Thy will, O My God (Psalm 40:7-8a).

*But with the precious blood of Christ, as of a lamb without blemish and without spot: who verily was foreordained **before the foundation of the world**...* (1 Peter 1:19-20).

It wasn't a surprise to Jesus exactly why He had come to earth—to be a sacrifice...

But this has all taken place that the writings of the prophets might be fulfilled [Jesus knew He was the fulfillment of all prophecy regarding the Messiah and the redemption of mankind] (Matthew 26:56a NIV).

To this end was I born, and for this cause came I into the world... [Does this sound like someone who would renege at the last minute?] (John 18:37b).

But I have a baptism to be baptized with; and how am I [pressed] *till it be accomplished!* [Does this sound like someone who would change His mind?] (Luke 12:50).

Christ knew from the beginning of time that as the Messiah He would be required to shed His blood and give His life (like the Old Testament sacrifices) and be rejected by the very people He had come to redeem. He knew mankind would reject Him; they had to. For Him to achieve His purpose, the people had to reject him. If they had loved Him, they would never have called for His crucifixion!

[Christ] *gave Himself for us, that He might redeem us from all iniquity...* (Titus 2:14a).

Unto Him that loved us, and washed us from our sins in His own blood (Revelation 1:5b).

If Jesus knew before He came to earth that as the Messiah *He was going to be beaten and sacrificed* for mankind's redemption and that He would have to take the sins of the whole world upon Himself (as did the goats under the Leviticus law), *then what else could it have been that prompted Him to ask God to "take away this cup" in Gethsemane?*

Now is My soul troubled; and what shall I say? Father, save Me from this hour: but for this cause came I unto this hour (John 12:27).

(But we are supposed to believe that in Gethsemane, at the eleventh hour, He changed His mind! That He didn't want to go the cross; He wanted the "cup" taken away.)

Consider that Jesus repeatedly told His disciples of His death and resurrection.

> *From that time forth began Jesus to show unto His disciples, how that He must go unto Jerusalem, and suffer many things of the elders and chief priests and scribes, and be killed, and be raised again the third day* (Matthew 16:21).

Jesus was very specific in this verse in Matthew. Therefore, when He asked God to take away the "cup" in Gethsemane, it is difficult to believe that He had not already considered the cost of taking upon Himself the sins of the world.

> *Then He took unto Him the twelve, and said unto them, Behold, we go up to Jerusalem, and all things that are written by the prophets concerning the Son of man shall be accomplished. For He shall be delivered unto the Gentiles, and shall be mocked, and spitefully entreated, and spitted on: and they shall scourge Him, and put Him to death: and the third day He shall rise again* (Luke 18:31-33).

Jesus knew exactly what was about to happen to Him and had known it from the beginning of time.

Again, we read in Luke 22:37a:

> *For I say unto you, that this that is written must yet be accomplished in Me.*

Nearer the time of His crucifixion, Jesus became more specific in His timing of events.

> *Ye know that **after two days** is the feast of the passover, and the Son of Man is betrayed to be crucified* (Matthew 26:2).

In Mark 14:30b, Jesus warned Peter that "***this night**, before the cock crow twice, thou shalt deny Me thrice*" (see also Matthew 26:34).

> *...**My time is at hand**; I will keep the passover at thy house with My disciples* (Matthew 26:18b).

*For in that she hath poured this ointment on My body, she did it **for** **My burial*** (Matthew 26:12; see also Mark 14:8).

When Jesus entered Jerusalem on a donkey, He knew without a doubt that His time of suffering was at hand. He told His disciples to organize the upper room for what became known as the "last supper." The countdown of events had already begun.

This was His purpose and destiny from the beginning.

Although the disciples didn't know, Jesus knew this was the last meal He would share with them. When He organized the last passover supper, He brought in the New Testament, and even predicted that Judas would betray Him and that Peter would deny Him after His arrest. He spoke of His broken body and spilt blood. It was no surprise to Him that He was about to be sacrificed. *It did not catch Him unaware.*

Following are the first keys in the final countdown.

1. Christ had forecast His impending death.

2. He had already allowed a woman to anoint Him for His burial.

3. He had brought in the New Testament, to supercede the Old Testament, and had instituted the breaking of bread, promising to have the fourth and final cup of wine with the resurrected saints in His Father's Kingdom.

The countdown for the crucifixion had begun.

Why then at the eleventh hour would Jesus change His mind in Gethsemane about enduring the cross, when He had already set in motion the sequence of events leading to the crucifixion?

Thinkest thou that I cannot now pray to My Father, and He shall presently give Me more than twelve legions of angels? But how then shall the scriptures be fulfilled, that thus it must be?...But all this was done that the scriptures of the prophets might be fulfilled (Matthew 26:53-54,56a).

Can you imagine the scene in Heaven? Can you see the angels who knew the *Word of God* in all His power and majesty? They had seen

Him come to earth and take on the role of a lowly carpenter, in a working-class household. This had puzzled them, knowing His former glory. But now, as they looked through the portals of Heaven, they could see *the Word* being beaten, mocked, and about to be crucified. I bet Michael, the warrior angel, was stomping up and down with a flaming sword in his hand, face set, and jaw tight, ready at the slightest indication from Jesus, to move at His command.

Can you see Gabriel, a look of unbelief and horror on his face as mankind manhandled their precious God? Imagine when the soldiers were abusing Jesus. He had only to nod His head at the awaiting heavenly host of angels, and myriads of them would have sprung to His defense. And the entire world would have been wiped out...in a moment of time!

But Jesus had made His decision long before He had been born in a stable.

> *Salvation is found in no one else, for there is no other name under heaven given to men by which we must be saved* (Acts 4:12 NIV).

So what was Jesus "sorrowing" for in the Garden of Gethsemane to cause Him to sweat great globules of blood? He could have stopped His death at any time, the angels being only too eager to come to His assistance. We have established that it was no surprise to Him that He would be sacrificed for the sins and sicknesses of the world. So then, what was the "cup" He wanted God to take away?

The Holy Spirit directed me to the Book of John, and I read the first few chapters. Jesus had been giving *instructions, admonishing and comforting* the disciples, and He continually warned the disciples of His impending death. It would be good now to read through the entire Book of John, but for expediency's sake, I will pick out the odd Scripture to highlight God's explanation to me.

From the Gospel of John, try to get the flow of where Jesus was heading and what was on His heart at this time.

> *I am the good shepherd; the good shepherd giveth his life for the sheep....Therefore doth My Father love Me, because I lay down My life, that I may take it again. No man **taketh** it from Me, but I lay it*

27

down of Myself. I have power to lay it down, and I have power to take it again... [This showed that He was fully in control of what was about to happen on Calvary] (John 10:11,17-18).

He continued to advise the disciples.

*And I, **if I be lifted up from the earth**, will draw all men unto Me. This He said signifying what death He should die* (John 12:32-33).

*Let not your heart be troubled: ye believe in God, believe also in Me. In My Father's house are many mansions: if it were not so, I would have told you. **I go to prepare a place for you**. And if I go and prepare a place for you, I will come again, and receive you unto Myself; that where I am, there ye may be also* (John 14:1-3).

*Verily, verily, I say unto you, He that believeth on Me, the works that I do shall he do also; and greater works than these shall he do; **because I go unto My Father**. And whatsoever ye shall ask in My name, that will I do, that the Father may be glorified in the Son. **If ye shall ask anything in My name, I will do it*** (John 14:12-14).

He was showing the disciples a new way. He knew He was leaving and wanted to show the disciples that their needs would still be met, by asking the Father for them...*in His name.*

*I will pray the Father, and He shall give you another Comforter, that He may abide with you for ever....I will not leave you comfortless: I will come to you. Yet a little while, and the world **seeth me no more**; but ye see Me: because I live, ye shall live also* (John 14:16,18-19).

Here Jesus promised to send the Holy Spirit to comfort and guide them. He promised not to leave them on their own.

*Peace I leave with you, My peace I give unto you: not as the world giveth, give I unto you. Let not your heart be troubled, neither let it be afraid. Ye have heard how I said unto you, **I go away**, and come again unto you. If ye loved Me, ye would rejoice, because I said, I go unto the Father: for My Father is greater than I. **And now I have told you before it come to pass**, that, when it is come to pass, ye might believe. Hereafter I will not talk much with you: for the prince of this world cometh, and hath nothing in Me. But that the* *world may know that I love the Father; and as the Father gave Me commandment, **even so I do**... (John 14:27-31).*

*Herein is My Father glorified, that ye bear much fruit; so shall ye be My disciples....If ye keep My commandments, ye shall abide in My love; even as I have kept My Father's commandments, and abide in His love....This is My commandment, That ye love one another, as I have loved you. Greater love hath no man than this, **that a man lay down his life for his friends** (John 15:8,10,12-13).*

*These things have I spoken unto you, that ye should not be offended. They shall put you out of the synagogues: yea, the time cometh, that whosoever killeth you will think that he doeth God service. And these things will they do unto you, because they have not known the Father, nor Me. But these things have I told you, that **when the time shall come**, ye may remember that I told you of them. And these things I said not unto you at the beginning, because I was with you (John 16:1-4).*

Whatsoever ye shall ask the Father in My name, He will give it you (John 16:23b).

In other words, instead of Jesus meeting the disciples' needs, they were to use *His* name, and the Father would do it. Christ had been available to the disciples for three years, ministering to them and supplying their every need, even paying taxes out of the mouth of fishes! He knew their strong points, and He knew their weak points. He knew Judas would betray Him. He knew Peter would deny Him, and the other disciples would scatter. He knew that later the disciples would suffer many persecutions and even death. Some would be stoned to death, some sawn in two, and another crucified upside down. As far as we know, John was the only one not martyred, but exiled on Patmos.

Jesus spent most of the Gospel of St. John reminding the disciples that He was about to be crucified, telling them to take their requests to the Father in His name, and encouraging them by saying that He would not leave them alone but send a Comforter to help them.

Jesus was distressed in spirit for the disciples when He entered Gethsemane. He knew when He left them, they would be comfortless, afraid, and would scatter during His trial and death. They would be at a loss and vulnerable without Him, so He tried to warn them and reassure them before the events began.

He had full knowledge of the sufferings and death He would endure on the cross, but *He hadn't reckoned on the terrible sorrow that would engulf Him at the prospect of leaving behind His beloved disciples who were so defenseless.*

> *"You will all fall away," Jesus told them, "for it is written: 'I will strike the shepherd, and the sheep will be scattered'"* (Mark 14:27 NIV).

> *...thou delightest not in burnt offering. The sacrifices of God are a broken spirit: a broken and a contrite heart, O God, Thou wilt not despise* (Psalm 51:16-17 KJV).

Jesus experienced a **broken heart***, right there at that time in history in the Garden of Gethsemane.*

Nothing had prepared Him for the special bond He had made with His disciples and followers. He had not reckoned on the heartache He would experience when He had to leave them behind. The sorrow of it engulfed Him.

It was a broken heart that was "the cup" that Jesus wanted God to "take away."

He would never have refused to go to the cross. Before time began, He knew the price He would have to pay to redeem mankind. But how could He have been prepared for the heartache of leaving these defenseless disciples behind? How could He possibly have experienced a broken heart beforehand? There are no broken hearts in Heaven! And the thought of leaving these vulnerable disciples overwhelmed Him after experiencing the human bond and love that was only available by being in human form. God's love of mankind was without limit, but this was love, eyeball to eyeball, with His creation that He had never experienced before.

Have you ever planned to go on a trip and prepared a list of instructions to give to those left behind? Isn't this exactly what Jesus did in the Book of John?

For He said, Surely they are My people, children that will not lie: so He was their Savior. In all their affliction He was afflicted, and the Angel of His presence saved them: in His love and in His pity He redeemed them... (Isaiah 63:8-9a).

He hath sent Me to bind up the brokenhearted... (Isaiah 61:1b).

(This was Jesus' time to experience a broken heart.) He now had firsthand experience of our grief and a broken heart because He experienced it Himself. He was deeply concerned for His disciples being scattered and killed. This feeling was something He could never have experienced in Heaven. He had to experience it firsthand on earth, and His love for the disciples overwhelmed Him.

Doesn't it strike you as odd that when Jesus was praying in Matthew 26, just prior to entering the Garden of Gethsemane, He kept coming back to the sleeping disciples and chastising them. In verse 41, Jesus said to the disciples, *"Watch and pray so that **you will not fall into temptation"*** (NIV). And in Mark 14:38, *"Watch and pray so that **you will not fall into temptation**. The spirit is willing, but the body is weak"* (NIV).

In very plain language He admonished Peter, *"Simon, Simon, satan has asked to sift you as wheat. But I have prayed for you, Simon, that your faith may not fail. And when you have turned back, strengthen your brothers"* (Luke 22:31-32 NIV).

Jesus was deeply concerned for the believers.

Let's tie up this revelation by the sequence of verses given to me in explanation and verification.

John chapter 17 should be read in its entirety; however, I will choose a few verses to amplify my point.

*These words spake Jesus, and lifted up His eyes to heaven, and said, Father, **the hour is come**; glorify Thy Son, that Thy Son may glorify Thee....I have glorified Thee on the earth: I have finished the work which Thou gavest Me to do....I have manifested Thy name unto the men which Thou gavest Me out of the world: Thine they were, and Thou gavest them Me; and they have kept Thy word....For I have given unto them the words which Thou gavest Me; and they have received them, and have known surely that I* *came out from Thee, and they have believed that Thou didst send Me. I pray for them: I pray not for the world, but for them which Thou hast given Me; for they are Thine. And all Mine are Thine, and Thine are Mine; and I am glorified in them. And now I am no more in the world, **but these are in the world**, and I come to Thee. Holy Father, keep through Thine own name those whom Thou hast given Me, that they may be one, as we are. While I was with them in the world, I kept them in Thy name: those that Thou gavest Me I have kept, and none of them is lost, but the son of perdition; that the scripture might be fulfilled....I have given them Thy word; and the world hath hated them, because they are not of the world, even as I am not of the world. I pray not that Thou shouldest take them out of the world, but that Thou shouldest keep them from the evil. They are not of the world, even as I am not of the world....As Thou hast sent Me into the world, even so have I also sent them into the world....Neither pray I for these alone, but for them also which shall believe on Me through their word; that they all may be one; as Thou, Father, art in Me, and I in Thee, that they also may be one in us: that the world may believe that Thou hast sent Me. And the glory which Thou gavest Me I have given them; that they may be one, even as we are one: I in them, and Thou in Me, that they may be made perfect in one; and that the world may know that Thou hast sent Me, and hast loved them, as Thou hast loved Me. Father, I will that they also, whom Thou hast given Me, be with Me where I am; that they may behold My glory, which Thou hast given Me: for Thou lovedst Me before the foundation of the world. O righteous Father, the world hath not known Thee: but I have known Thee, and these have known that Thou hast sent Me. And I have declared unto them Thy name, and will declare it: that the love wherewith Thou hast loved Me may be in them, and I in them* (John 17:1,4,6,8-12,14-16,18,20-26).

What would you say was paramount on Christ's mind after this prayer to His Father?

The believers, His disciples, the ones whom He had lived and shared everything with. His relationship with them was about to end, and He knew the price they would have to pay for knowing Him.

Jesus was very distressed about having to leave the disciples during this time of His imprisonment and death. He knew what would happen to them, their ultimate fate, and He asked the Father to take away *this sorrow* that was breaking His heart. Also see Matthew 26:37-38.

What would your pastor do if the government told him that every member of his congregation, who would not denounce their faith, would be shot the next morning? He'd be on his knees all night praying for each of them, just as Jesus had done in Gethsemane!

Read the next verse that follows after Jesus had been praying for His disciples in John chapter 17,

> *When Jesus had spoken these words, He went forth with His disciples over the brook Cedron, where was a garden* [Gethsemane], *into the which He entered, and His disciples* (John 18:1).

We have established that the believers were *utmost in Christ's mind when He went into the Garden of Gethsemane.* He took those three who were closest to Him, and as He realized what was ahead for each of the believers, His heart *broke for them.* Subsequently, He asked the Father to "take away this cup."

He had always known He would have the cross to face, but nothing had prepared Him for the intense love He felt towards the believers and how protective He would feel at His leaving.

In Gethsemane, Jesus lifted up every disciple and believer in prayer and *every believer since then.* He interceded for the believers then, and He is still doing so today at the right hand of the Father.

CONTRA-ARGUMENT

An explanation given regarding what happened in Gethsemane states that Jesus emptied Himself of all godliness when He came to earth, and it was His humanity that caused Him to ask God to take away the "cup" when He thought of the cross and mankind's sins upon Him, which would separate Him from God.

It is true that Jesus emptied Himself of His godliness when He was made man, but to say that His humanity caused Him to fear death and the sins of the world being poured on Him, which in turn made Him ask the Father to take the "cup" away, is not true.

Every believer who was thrown to the lions in the Coliseum in Rome, every believer who refused to follow papal doctrine and was burnt at the stake for their beliefs, every martyr throughout time who has paid for his or her belief in God with their lives, was just as human as Jesus Christ. *But being human does not necessarily make you a coward, as all the martyrs through the ages have proved.*

When Adam sinned and broke his intimate relationship with God, Jesus knew that as the Messiah He would be sacrificed to reconcile man to God. Before He left His heavenly realm, He knew that this was to be the purpose for Him coming into the world in man form. The cross was not a surprise to Jesus. He knew He would be sacrificed to take away the sins of man, and He must have known *then* that sin would separate Him from God.

It is inconceivable to think He hadn't counted the cost of this act. And apparently, He felt the cost would be worth it. So, being fore-warned with that knowledge, why would He ask the Father to take "the cup" (of going to the cross) from Him only a few hours before He went to the cross?

What would have been the purpose of Him coming into the world at all?

Just suppose that Jesus really had asked to have "the cross and sins of mankind taken away from Him" in Gethsemane as we are led to believe...and our heavenly Father had said, "yes" to His request to take away "the cup of suffering." What would have been the point in Jesus coming to the earth in the first place?

Where would that have left mankind? How can we continue to believe that the promised Messiah wanted to back out at the last moment? The whole message of the Bible would have been nullified.

It was Adam's weakness that got us into sin, so what good was this Messiah if He too showed weakness and cowardice at the last minute? How can we believe that for one solitary moment Jesus would have considered backing out of His very purpose for coming to earth?

CONFIRMATION

The final seal on this revelation is that Jesus was still in the Garden of Gethsemane—in fact, it was shortly after He had asked God to "take away this cup"—when the soldiers arrived to arrest Him. Peter became angry and cut off a man's ear, and surprisingly Jesus said to Peter in John 18:11, *"Put your sword away! Shall I not drink the cup the Father has given Me?"* (NIV).

Now if Calvary and the cross was the "cup" that Jesus wanted taken away only minutes before, He would have been very hypocritical to have reprimanded Peter for trying to stop the sequence of events that were to follow.

This was His destiny—the very purpose for His humanity and His mission to earth. There would have been no reason to visit earth otherwise.

Our minds can't comprehend the consequences had God answered "yes" if His request had been to not go to the cross or take the sins of the world upon Himself. It's too horrific to contemplate.

Jesus knew all too well the will of the Father, and He knew His destiny—to reconcile man to God. And on the cross, He said to God, *"It is finished."* In other words, *"Mission accomplished!"*

So, establish in your hearts, that when Jesus asked the Father to take away this "cup of sorrow" in Gethsemane, He was not backing out of the pain and humiliation He was about to face on the cross, nor attempting to avoid the inevitable separation from the Father when the sins of the whole world were poured out on Him. Nothing so selfish or cowardly ever crossed His mind.

This was the reason He had come to earth. This was the Father's will that He had gladly submitted to.

And at the same time, He loved the *believers* so much that it was the distress and hardship that *they* would endure that was breaking His heart and making Him "sorrowful, as unto death."

Jesus never had a selfish bone in His body; He was not thinking about Himself in Gethsemane. Rather, His tremendous love for His followers caused great drops of blood to pour from His brow.

...That's how much Jesus loves you.

Having established the great love that the Godhead has for mankind, we understand what a heritage we have to maintain and how important it is to hold the ground that the Lord Jesus has paid so dearly for on Calvary. The only way to do that is to learn what the Bible says about our enemy...even the smallest detail. This will give us the advantage to deal with his nature, strategy, and purpose in his opposition to the Godhead and the believers. Our Commander in Chief paid a dear price for our salvation. We owe it to Him not only to know about the character of evil and his tactics, but to recognize what weapons we have been given in order to become overcomers and hold the ground that Jesus established by His death, until the return of our Savior.

If you want to become part of this glorious army but have never accepted Christ as your personal Savior or known His wonderful grace and forgiveness, you need to say the following prayer.

Heavenly Father, I desire to be Your child, and I ask forgiveness for my sins. I acknowledge Jesus Christ is the Son of God, and that He died that my sins might be forgiven. From this day onward, I receive Him as my Savior, and I walk in the power of your Holy Spirit, with a heart that desires to serve You and become an overcomer. Thank You for my salvation and the peace and joy in my heart. Amen.

2

KNOWING THE ENEMY

If you were drafted into the army and arrived at boot camp, you would never expect upon being issued a uniform and given a gun, to be commanded to go immediately "somewhere over the ridge" and annihilate the enemy— *without first being thoroughly and properly trained.*

There could be a whole armory of weapons for you to use for this purpose, but until you knew how to work the weapons, and what weapons to use in which circumstances, the weapons would be no more than a pile of metal and totally useless to you. On the other hand, it would be just as ineffective if you had a good knowledge of weaponry, yet didn't know who your enemy was, his location, his strength, or his tactics. It would be impossible to make war against him. The most you could do in those circumstances would be to stage a defensive action when you came under attack from him. For without a thorough knowledge of your enemy and a complete knowledge of weaponry available to you, you have no means of attacking him and overcoming him...and that's the plight of many of God's people today.

Ask the average Christian if he is part of the Lord's glorious army, and you will get an affirmative answer. Ask him what his last battle was like, and he will probably tell you that when the enemy attacked him with a problem or sickness, he stood firm and overcame the enemy by faith. Now, this reply is not wrong, but at the most, it is just a mediocre attempt at a defensive action against an *attack* from satan. And it is not worthy of the glorious triumphant army that Christ is expecting to find when He returns.

The Bible says that "the gates of hell shall not prevail against it [God's army]" (Matt. 16:18b), meaning, satan's kingdom will not be able to stand against the *onslaught* of the army of God.

We are called to be *overcomers*...not *defenders*! The Church has been given a command by our Commander in Chief, Jesus Christ, that we are to be overcomers, a triumphant Church, without spot or wrinkle, and to be able and ready to plunder satan's kingdom, crashing down the gates of hell.

On the cross at Calvary, Jesus triumphed over satan and his hordes (see Col. 2:15). We, the Church, have been left with the mandate to do the same. But we can't do it if we are unprepared to do battle because we are lacking in knowledge. We have to *attack* the works of the enemy and pull down the strongholds *he* has already established, reclaim them, and stop *him* from taking any new territory.

For too long, satan has deceived the world into thinking that this planet is under his authority. Jesus paid a dear price so that *mankind* could reclaim this authority. Only *unbelievers* give satan the legal right to have authority over them. But Christians *have authority, delegated by Jesus Christ, for them to rule*; and they don't have to accept anything from satan's hands.

John 12:31b says, *"Now shall the prince of this world be cast out."* God has never intended for us to be victims; He has other plans for believers.

> *I will bring forth a seed out of...Judah* [Jesus] *an inheritor of My mountains* [the Messiah]*: and Mine elect* [Christian believers] *shall inherit it* [earth]*, and My servants shall dwell there* (Isaiah 65:9).

The earth has been given back to mankind by Christ's sacrifice, as it was originally given to Adam in the beginning. Adam was neither sick, nor poor, nor had any problems until he chose to obey and follow satan, through the mouth of the snake, in the Garden of Eden. So, since our Savior, Jesus Christ, gave His life as a sacrifice for mankind, every believer, in essence, now has ownership of *all* that Adam had before he fell into disobedience and disgrace. Any sickness or works of the enemy that try to adversely influence our lives should be dealt with immediately.

But this is a normal skirmish. We have to learn how to attack too!

To fight, we have to know the ways of our enemy. To go in and attack him unaware, take advantage of his weak spots, and fight him with the most sophisticated equipment that God can supply...and overcome him in every town and city, until he flees at the sight of God's army!

The prophet Joel foresaw this end-time glorious army and prophesied that we should:

Blow ye the trumpet in Zion, and sound an alarm in My holy mountain: let all the inhabitants of the land tremble: for the day of the Lord cometh, for it is nigh at hand...a great people and a strong [God's army]; there hath not been ever the like, neither shall be any more after it, even to the years of many generations. A fire devoureth before them; and behind them a flame burneth: the land is as the garden of Eden before them, and behind them a desolate wilderness; yea, and nothing shall escape them. The appearance of them is as the appearance of horses; and as horsemen, so shall they run. Like the noise of chariots on the tops of mountains shall they leap, like the noise of a flame of fire that devoureth the stubble, as a strong people set in battle array. Before their face the people shall be much pained: all faces shall gather blackness. They shall run like mighty men; they shall climb the wall like men of war; and they shall march every one on his ways, and they shall not break their ranks; neither shall one thrust another [unity in the body]; they shall walk every one in his path: and when they fall upon the sword, they shall not be wounded [supernatural protection]. They shall run to and fro in the city; they shall run upon the wall, they shall climb up upon the houses; they shall enter in at the windows like a thief [nowhere for satan to hide]. The earth shall quake before them; the heavens shall tremble [as satan's kingdom is invaded].... *And the Lord shall utter His voice before His army: for His camp is very great...* (Joel 2:1,2b-10a,11a).

To be an effective member of this army, the first thing we have to do is gain a thorough knowledge of our enemy. We can't *see him*, for he is in spirit form. So let's look into the heavenlies and discover what beings inhabit the spiritual realm. We will go into the smallest detail, for there is nothing about the enemy that we want to miss. A thorough knowledge of him means that at no time can he do something unexpected or something we cannot handle. Like any good soldier, we have to both anticipate and detect his movements. Couple the power of the Holy Spirit with the knowledge already given to us in the Word of God...*and the gates of hell will not prevail against us!*

THE HEAVENLIES

Genesis 1:1 says, *"In the beginning, God created...."* Everything that exists on the earth and in the heavens was created originally by God. God created the spirit beings, angels and archangels, and had an orderly heavenly system operating in Heaven.

Among the chief angels, the Bible refers mainly to three by name:

▸ Gabriel—who stands before God.

▸ Michael—the angelic prince responsible for Israel.

▸ Lucifer—the most beautiful of all angels.

In the beginning, lucifer was made a ruler/guardian of our planet Earth, with the commission from God to prepare the earth for God's most precious possession—mankind.

Sometime, during his earthly rule, as lucifer prepared the earth for mankind to inhabit, pride filled his heart. He liked the feel of authority and decided he would like to rule permanently. He even thought he might take over God's Kingdom! He stupidly made an attempt to overthrow God, and he was promptly relieved of his position of overseer of the earth and flung back to earth where he now makes himself the pseudo-ruler.

Apart from the ordinary angels (the term "ordinary angels" is used to differentiate between them and archangels and later, fallen angels), there are other spirit beings in the heavens: seraphim (see Isa. 6:2,6); cherubim (see Gen. 3:24; Ezek. 5:1-26); spirit animals [shaped like fleshly ones on earth] (see Rev. 19:11-19); living creatures (see Rev. 4:6); and, of course, the 24 elders that surround God's throne, praising Him night and day (see Rev. 5:14). Also mentioned in the Bible are the spirit princes of Persia and Greece (see Dan. 10:13,20) and dragons (see Rev. 12:3-4), and lastly, demons and demon locust (see Rev. 9:1-11).

ANGELS

For our purposes, we will conduct a closer study of the angels.

They live in a spiritual realm. Angels, in appearance, are like you and me, with all the same body parts as mankind (see Gen. 18:2,4,8; 19:1-22). They have feelings and emotions like us.

- ▸ They can sin (see Gen. 6:1-4; Jude 6-7).

- ▸ They can lust after forbidden flesh (see Jude 6-7).

- ▸ They can cook (see 1 Kings 19:5-7).

- ▸ They get hungry (see Gen. 18:8; 19:3).

- ▸ They are intelligent and have wisdom (see 2 Sam. 14:20).

- ▸ They are strong and mighty, modest, meek and patient (see 2 Pet. 2:11; Num. 22:22-35).

- ▸ They operate in both the spiritual and material realms. And although invisible in the earthly realm, they can, with God's permission, appear visible to humans (see Gen. 18:2; 22:11; 2 Kings 19:35; Acts 1:10; 12:7-10).

- ▸ They ascend and descend to Heaven (see Gen. 28:12; John 1:51).

- ▸ They are immortal (see Rev. 8:13).

- ▸ They are much larger than us and have powerful and mighty bodies (see 2 Thess. 1:7-10; Rev. 18:1; Isa. 37:36).

- ▸ Angels, like humans, are given a "free will" to obey God or rebel against Him.

- ▸ They can be angry (see Rev. 12:12).

- ▸ They can be filled with pride (see Ezek. 28:17; 1 Tim. 3:6).

- ▸ They can be hostile (see Gen. 3:15).

- ▸ They have passions (see Gen. 6:1-4).

- ▸ Angels can seek revenge on mankind (see 1 Pet. 5:8).

Those who chose to torment man, ultimately in due course, became the "fallen angels."

THE ARCHANGELS

Gabriel ministers to God. He is used in areas of great responsibility in bringing God's plan to mankind; he obeys God unconditionally (see Dan. 8:16-19; 9:20-23; 10:8-11; Luke 1:19,26).

Michael is the spiritual prince of Israel. Israel, being referred to as the wife of God, is very important to him, and responsibility of Israel is given to him (see Dan. 10:13,21; Jude 9; Rev. 12:7-9).

Note that every nation or country has an angel appointed by God to oversee it.

Lucifer was supposedly the most beautiful and wisest of the archangels, though it is difficult to understand how he can claim to be wise and still be so presumptuous as to set himself up against God. But in any case, he did. Sometime, as he was preparing the earth for mankind to inhabit, pride filled lucifer's heart, and he made an attempt to overthrow God. He was promptly relieved of his position as overseer of the earth and now makes himself the pseudo-ruler of man's dominion on earth.

As the archangels, Gabriel and Michael, continued to minister to and serve God, lucifer had some plans of his own. God had appointed him to rule over the original planet Earth and to prepare it for mankind. The following Scripture confirms his original designation and location.

Lucifer

*How art thou fallen from heaven, O Lucifer, son of the morning! how art thou cut down to the ground, which didst weaken the nations! For thou hast said in thine heart, **I will** ascend into heaven, **I will exalt my** throne above the stars of God: **I will** sit also upon the mount of the congregation, in the sides of the north: I will ascend above the heights of the clouds: **I will** be like the most High (Isaiah 14:12-14).*

Lucifer must have been located under Heaven to begin with, as he determined in his heart to *ascend* into Heaven, and also *under* the stars, as he wanted to exalt his throne *above* them. Note that he had already been given a "throne." One who sits on a throne, rules; and only God could have given him that authority...in the beginning! The fact that *clouds* surround only the planet Earth and no other planet and that lucifer wanted to *ascend* above them, means he must have been situated *below* them in the beginning. This evidence locates his temporary rule to earth.

God gave lucifer the responsibility of preparing the original earth for mankind. Remember, the Bible says lucifer was "full of wisdom," so it would have been well within his ability to undertake the designated task. God gave him angels and other spirit beings to help him complete the earth in readiness for the creation nearest to God's heart—mankind.

During his reign, lucifer liked the feeling of power he exercised over his team of workers. He took great pride in his accomplishments and ability, and then he started trafficking in slander against God. He must have been pretty persuasive because he convinced a third, not all, of the angels that were working with him, to follow him in his attempt to take over God's throne.

Son of man, take up a lamentation upon the king of Tyrus, and say unto him, Thus saith the Lord God; Thou sealest up the sum, full of wisdom, and perfect in beauty. Thou hast been in Eden the garden of God [spiritual garden]; every precious stone was thy covering, the sardius, topaz, and the diamond, the beryl, the onyx, the jasper, the sapphire, the emerald, and the carbuncle, and gold: the workmanship of thy tabrets and of thy pipes [music] *was prepared in thee in the day that thou was created. Thou art the anointed cherub that covereth; and I* [God] **have set thee so** [preparing the earth for mankind]*; thou wast upon the holy mountain of God; thou hast walked up and down in the midst of the stones of fire. Thou wast perfect in thy ways from the day that thou was created, till* **iniquity was found in thee. By the multitude of thy merchandise they have filled the midst of thee with violence, and thou hast sinned**: *therefore I will cast thee as profane out of the mountain of God: and I will destroy thee, O covering cherub, from the midst of the stones of fire. Thine heart was lifted up because of thy beauty, thou hast corrupted thy wisdom by reason of thy brightness: I will cast thee to the ground, I will lay thee before kings, that they may behold thee. Thou hast defiled thy sanctuaries by the multitude of thine iniquities, by the iniquity of thy traffic* [in slander]*; therefore will I bring forth a fire from the midst of thee, it shall devour thee, and I will bring thee to ashes upon the earth in the sight of all them that behold thee* (Ezekiel 28:12-18).

The king of Tyrus, described in this Ezekiel Scripture, was both an earthly ruler and a spiritual ruler. The earthly ruler had inherited his kingdom by the death of his father and could never have been in the spiritual, bejeweled "garden of God." We, therefore, have to acknowledge that we are also talking about a spiritual ruler of Tyrus (see verse 13), i.e. lucifer. He had access to the Garden of Eden and walked upon the holy mountain of God; but an earthly ruler could not have done this.

These verses tell us that God Himself placed lucifer as guardian/protector, to overshadow the earth ("covereth"—verse 14). God's Word says, "I have set thee so."

But lucifer, filled with pride and ambition, slandered God and sinned. Isaiah 14:13-15 reveals that he said in his heart, *"I will ascend into heaven."* And he must have worked deceitfully and persuasively to get a third of the angels to follow him and rebel against God.

"*I will exalt my throne above the stars of God.*" There is no mistaking that lucifer intended to dethrone God and make himself the supreme ruler.

"*I will also sit upon the mount of the congregation, in the sides of the north.*" God's Kingdom is always referred to as being on "the sides of the north." So, lucifer was not content to merely rule the earth; he wanted to overthrow God and take over *His throne*! God's reaction to this rebellion was to cast him out of Heaven (see Ezek. 28:17).

It was a bodily casting out by the power of Almighty God—"*How thou art cut down.*" The Hebrew word is *gada*—to cut down, like the felling of a tree, to totally cut off.

We can take from this that lucifer was stopped on his way to God's throne and was instantly cut off, cast down, and thrown back to the earth, on which he had his throne, before he committed such an act of sedition and treason towards God. It cost him his name (he is now known as satan), and it cost him his place in Heaven.

What could God do about the rebellious situation? He had given lucifer a throne and a planet to prepare...but this rebellion could not continue. God did the only thing He could do in the circumstances— He obliterated the earth. He made the earth "chaos." He made it "without form and void," leaving lucifer bereft of a kingdom and a throne on which to rule. "*...and darkness was upon the face of the deep*" (Gen. 1:2a).

3

EARTH'S ORIGINS

"In the beginning God created the heaven and the earth" (Gen. 1:1) is the original (lucifer's) earth and heaven, created by God, with lucifer as the "guardian cherub," preparing the earth for God's creation—mankind. *"And the earth was without form, and void"* (Gen. 1:2a) is the same earth after God made lucifer's earth formless and empty.

It is impossible that God was referring to a single creation of the earth. Because once God had "created earth," it would have *had both form and substance*, and not been *"without form, and void."*

In verse 1 of Genesis chapter 1, the Hebrew word, *bara*, is used, which means "to create." Also, note in Genesis 1:2b, that waters were upon the face of the earth. Yet God called the earth "dry land" in verse 10. So the original earth must have had dry land as it was also called earth. So, how had the dry land become flooded? God had flooded it when He made it "chaotic" after the revolt of lucifer (*"...and the Spirit of God moved upon the face of the waters"* [Gen. 1:2b]).

These circumstances are confirmed in Second Peter 3:6-7:

47

*Whereby the world **that then was**, being overflowed with water, perished: but the heavens and the earth, **which are now**, by the same word are kept in store, reserved unto fire against the day of judgment and perdition of ungodly men.*

No one knows the time span between the first created earth and the second re-creation of earth, but when God was ready once again to re-create the earth, the Hebrew word, *asah*, is used, which means "to make out of existing material"—in readiness for mankind.

His Spirit moved over the waters of the original earth that had been flooded because of lucifer's rebellion. For a second time, God started to prepared the earth for His beloved creation, mankind (see Gen. 1:3-25). But this time, God put the authority and rulership of the earth directly into mankind's *own hands*, giving Adam "dominion," which meant *lordship, sovereignty, rulership*, and *predominance* over all the earth and over all the living things that had been put back onto earth to *replenish* it (see Gen. 1:28).

Note that the word *replenish* means "to stock or refill *again*" and not simply "*plenish*" the earth.

Can you imagine satan's reaction to Adam's rulership? Mankind had been put in control of the planet Earth this time. Subsequently, satan desperately wanted the earth back, to be ruler of it again.

It must be humiliating to have your authority and power taken from you, to be a ruler and have nowhere to rule! So, in his own inimitable style, he made a plan to visit the man beings, Adam and Eve, with the intention of taking the earth once again *under his control and rule*.

Knowing of lucifer's fall and his character, does it surprise you that, when working through the snake, he made his appearance in the Garden of Eden?

REBELLION IN THE GARDEN

Now the serpent was more crafty than any of the wild animals the Lord God had made [and was obviously prepared to be a part of satan's plan]. *He said to the woman, "Did God really say, 'You must not eat from any tree in the garden'?" The woman said to the serpent, "We may eat fruit from the trees in the garden, but God did say, 'You must not eat fruit from the tree that is in the middle of the garden, and you must not touch it, or you will die'"* (Genesis 3:1-3 NIV).

In Genesis chapter 3, satan, through the snake, instilled doubt in Eve regarding God's directives to Adam by saying, *"Hath God said?"* In verse 4, he openly contradicted God by saying, *"Ye shall not surely die."* He went on in verse 5, persuasively, to cause Adam and Eve to be disobedient to God, rebel, and fall from God's grace, by offering them the same reward that he himself so coveted when he tried to take over God's throne.

> *For God doth know that in the day ye eat thereof, then your eyes shall be opened, and ye shall be as gods, knowing good and evil* (Genesis 3:5).

We all know the story of how Eve fell for the deception of satan. And Adam, disregarding God's commands about the fruit of the tree of the knowledge of good and evil, *stood there right beside Eve* (see Gen. 3:6), as she ate the fruit. He not only watched his wife eat the forbidden fruit but also partook of the same himself! Eve was deceived, but Adam committed high treason by this act!

In the past, the man beings, Adam and Eve, had been obedient to God, served Him, and been wholly submitted to Him. He was their Master, over both of them and all they possessed.

Note that after Adam was created, God asked him to name all the animals. When you own something, you have the right to name it. Jesus, the "Word," was used to create the universe and spoke everything into existence; and this exercise of naming the animals was to show Adam that there was power in his spoken word too! By asking him to name all the animals, God showed Adam his authority and rulership in and over the earth.

These same man beings, to whom God had given rule over the new earth and dominion over all in it, now chose to obey and follow satan instead of God, making satan their new master. *You obey the one who has rule over you.* And if satan was master over the man beings, he was also master over all their possessions, including the planet Earth and everything in it! *Satan took possession of the earth, legally, when Adam submitted to him.*

Jesus, in the desert, verified this when satan offered Him *"all the kingdoms of the world."* Satan said unto Jesus, *"All this power will I give thee, and the glory of them: for that is delivered unto me* [by Adam]; *and I can give it to whosoever I want"* (Luke 4:5-6 KJV with author's paraphrase). Here was a good opportunity for Jesus to correct satan had the statement been untrue, but He never corrected him about ownership of the earth. He knew that satan had taken it from Adam and Eve—legally, *through their disobedience to God and obedience to him.* So once more, satan, a.k.a. lucifer, had rulership of planet Earth!

However, there was still one thing bothering satan. In Genesis 3:15, God pronounced His judgment upon both man beings for their disobedience and upon the snake that had always stood so tall. The snake was humbled and left to slither in the dust of the ground forevermore.

Satan was not concerned what judgment was passed on the man beings or the snake. What did concern him was the promise that God gave to Adam and Eve. *"I will put enmity between thee* [the snake] *and the woman* [obviously, there had been no enmity between them before, because Eve had not been afraid to speak to the snake], *and between thy seed and her seed* [between the children of God and the adopted children of the snake—satan's]" (Gen. 3:15a).

God knew who was behind the cunning reptile, and He spoke directly to satan. *"...he will crush your head..."* (Gen. 3:15b NIV). That's how you kill a snake. So, God was showing satan that he would be totally crushed by the *seed of man.* It was God's promise of a Savior for mankind, the first mention of a Messiah...and a glimpse of satan's ultimate fate.

To the man He said, *"...and thou shalt bruise his heel"* (Gen. 3:15b). A bruise on the heel can be excruciatingly painful for a while...but it does heal. And Jesus Christ was mortally wounded and suffered tremendous pain on the cross...*for a while*, until His resurrection. Praise God!

SATAN'S PLAN

When God made this promise in Genesis chapter 3, I believe that satan made a hasty retreat from the Garden of Eden back to his cohorts, the fallen angels, who had joined him in rebelling against God. They put their heads together to see what they could do to foil this promise that God had made to mankind through Adam and Eve, to produce the Messiah through the seed of the man!

Satan decided to organize himself properly, working *his* heavenly system in the same way that God ran His. He knew the system worked for God, so he set up his own new kingdom in a similar way.

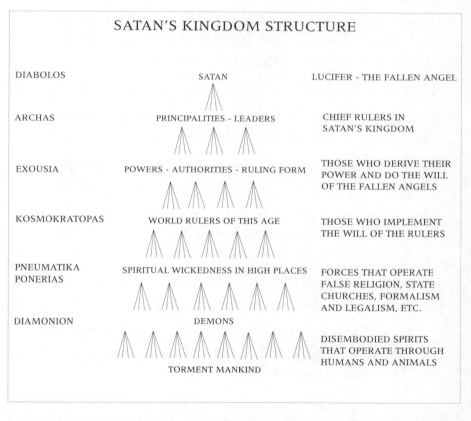

Principalities (Archas): Chief ruling, fallen angels of the highest rank under satan. They have similar duties to the archangels in God's Kingdom (see Rom. 8:38; Eph. 1:21; 3:10; 6:12; and Col. 2:10,15).

Authorities (Excousias): These authorities make sure the commands of satan are carried through the ranks, by executing the orders of the chief rulers. Their duties are similar to the ordinary angels in God's Kingdom (see 1 Cor. 15:24; Eph..6:12; 1 Pet. 3:22).

Rulers of the darkness of this world (Kosmokratopas): The spirit world rulers of continents, nations, cities, and towns (see Eph. 6:12).

Spiritual wickedness in high places (Pneumatika Ponerias): Spiritual forces that inhabit the sphere above the earth and that form the great state churches, legalism, traditionalism, and the apostate churches, and all false religions and cults (see Eph:1:21, 6:12).

Demons (Diamonion and Diamon): evil spirits, disembodied spirits, operating through man or animals; the demonic tormenters of mankind, especially the Christian believers.

Note that Jesus Christ defeated all of the above entities on the cross.

And having spoiled principalities and powers, He made a show of them openly, triumphing over them in it (Colossians 2:15).

Who is gone into heaven, and is on the right hand of God; angels and authorities and powers being made subject unto Him (1 Peter 3:22).

For we wrestle not against flesh and blood, but against principalities, against powers, against the rulers of the darkness of the world, against spiritual wickedness in high places (Ephesians 6:12).

Having set up his kingdom, satan turned his attention back to the problem of the promised Messiah for mankind.

And I will put enmity between thee and the woman, and between thy seed and her seed; it shall bruise thy head, and thou shalt bruise his heel (Genesis 3:15).

After satan had had an exhausting board meeting with his principalities—the fallen angels, it was decided that if they were going to avoid having their *"head crushed,"* they would somehow have to stop or pollute the *"seed of the woman"* so as to prevent the arrival of the promised Messiah. After great deliberation, they formulated their plan.

*And it came to pass, when men began to multiply on the face of the earth, and daughters were born unto them, that the **sons of** God saw the **daughters of** men that they were fair; and they took them wives of all which they chose. And the Lord said, My spirit shall not always strive with man, for that he also is flesh; yet his days shall be an hundred and twenty years. There were **giants** in the earth in those days; and also after that, when the **sons of God** came in unto the **daughters of men**, and they bare **children** to them, the same became mighty men which were of old, men of renown. And God saw that the wickedness of man was great on the earth, and that every imagination of the thoughts of his heart was only evil continually* (Genesis 6:1-5).

Notice the two distinct expressions here—the *"sons of God"* and the *"daughters of men."* This indicates two different species—one a product of *God*, the other a product of *man*.

*Now there was a day when the **sons of** God came to present themselves before the Lord, and satan came also among them* (Job 1:6).

*Again there was a day when the **sons of God** came to present themselves before the Lord, and satan came also among them to present himself before the Lord* (Job 2:1).

*When the morning stars sang together, and all the **sons of God** shouted for joy?* (Job 38:7)

The "sons of God" were angels who presented themselves before God in Heaven within the heavenly realm. Humans cannot present themselves in God's throne room. In these Scriptures, satan came into the throne room with the angels. Notice the devil is referred to as "satan" and not "lucifer," as he had already lost his name and his place in Heaven through his rebellion.

These angels sinned because they did not keep their first estate, or to their own realm. In other words, they were created originally by God to minister to Him, and to keep and operate within their own realm in the heavenlies, unless requested by Him to do otherwise. These fallen angels came down to earth and transversed the laws of the universe by having sexual relations with *"the daughters of men"*—from the heavenly realm into the human realm, which was forbidden by God.

The reason they did this was to spoil the "pure" Adamite (human) bloodline, and thus prevent the promised "seed of the woman" (the *Messiah*), from coming into the world to defeat satan's new rulership of earth.

So, these angels had sexual relationships (*"took them wives of all which they chose"*) with the "daughters of men" and produced "giants."

Now, think for a moment. Cast your mind forward for a comparison illustration of the implication of this ungodly union. Compare it with the virgin birth of Jesus Christ.

> ...*Fear not, Mary: for thou hast found favor with God. And, behold, thou shalt conceive in thy womb, and bring forth a son, and shalt call His name Jesus. He shall be great, and shall be called the Son of the Highest: and the Lord God shall give unto Him the throne of His father David: and He shall reign over the house of Jacob for ever; and of His kingdom there shall be no end. Then said Mary unto the angel, How shall this be, seeing I know not a man?* (Luke 1:30-34)

Mary clearly stated that she knew "no man" (see verse 34). But Gabriel had been sent by God to tell her:

> ...*The Holy Ghost shall come upon thee, and the power of the Highest shall overshadow thee: therefore also that* **holy** *thing which shall be born of thee shall be called the Son of God* (Luke 1:35).

Although through her humanity Mary produced a human child, nonetheless, the child was *conceived supernaturally by the "power of the Highest,"* and the child became a *"holy thing,"* and was to be called the "Son of God," in fact, Jesus Christ our Savior. The Holy Ghost sired our Savior, and Mary conceived Him.

Now, consider what the result of a supernatural *unholy* conception would produce!

Keeping in mind that Jesus was in human form, but was *"holy,"* He took on the nature of God, His Father. Then consider the result of the union between the fallen angels and the daughters of men. They might have produced a child in human form (even though they were giant size), but they took on the nature of *their* fathers! They were as *unholy* and as *evil* as were their fathers, the fallen angels!

54

The seed of mankind was polluted!

God's reaction to mankind for his part in this unnatural union with the fallen angels is stated in Genesis 6:6-7:

> *And it repented the Lord that He had made man on the earth, and it grieved Him at His heart. And the Lord said, I will destroy man whom I have created from the face of the earth; both man, and beast, and the creeping thing, and the fowls of the air; for it repenteth Me that I have made them.*

The giants' evil seeds began to multiply!

4

GOD'S RESCUE MISSION

*But Noah found grace in the eyes of the Lord. These are the genera-
tions of Noah: Noah was a just man and **perfect** in his generations,
and Noah walked with God. And Noah begat three sons, Shem,
Ham, and Japheth. The earth also was corrupt before God, and the
earth was filled with violence* [influenced by the seed of fallen
angels]. *And God looked upon the earth, and, behold, it was corrupt; for all flesh had corrupted His way upon the earth. And God
said unto Noah, The end of all flesh is come before Me; for the earth
is filled with violence through them; and, behold, I will destroy
them with the earth* (Genesis 6:8-13).

The Hebrew word, *tamiym,* used in connection with Noah's *"perfect
in his generations,"* translated means, *"without blemish, pure stock, and bodily perfect."* This same word is used several times in the Old Testament in
referring to sacrificial animals that had to be "without blemish and of
pure stock." Noah and his family were chosen, not necessarily for the
godly life they were living, but because they were the only *"pure
Adamite bloodline"* family left. *All the other families must have been a mixture of both men and fallen angels.*

Their offspring, the giants, had fathered more offspring; and their offspring had fathered more offspring; and so on, until Noah's family had been the only family left unspoiled.

There is a very good reason that Genesis chapter 5 details the pure lineage from Adam to Noah—to prove that the "sons of God" and their ungodly union with mankind had not tainted the pure bloodline of the promised Messiah, Jesus Christ.

Satan had come to within eight persons of achieving his goal! However, he learned the hard way that God never fails in His mission!

And God sent a flood to cover the earth...

THE FLOODS

It is interesting to note a few basic differences about lucifer's flood and Noah's flood that occurred later.

In lucifer's flood, the earth was made formless and void; darkness was upon the face of the earth. All beings, vegetation, fish, animals, birds, and land were destroyed. We don't know how long the original earth ruled by lucifer was under water, but it took God's Spirit only one moment in time to lift the waters off it.

But in Noah's flood, the earth was not left formless. It still had substance and was occupied (eight persons). All things were preserved— animals (on the ark), vegetation, fish, and bird life; and the flood lasted just over a year before the waters abated.

I beheld the earth, and, lo, it was without form, and void; and the heavens, and they had no light (Jeremiah 4:23).

*Whereby the world that **then was**, being overflowed with water, perished: but the heavens and the earth, **which are now**, by the same word are kept in store, reserved unto fire against the day of judgment and perdition of ungodly men (2 Peter 3:6-7).*

Unlike lucifer's flood, once Noah and his family were on dry land, and the waters abated, there had been no need for any re-creative miracles to bring the land back into its original state. The vegetation grew again. The animals and birds in the ark with Noah had been spared, and the sea life was intact. God told Noah to *"replenish"* the earth, using the same word He had previously used to instruct Adam when He had re-created the earth.

Again, God put His trust in mankind, hoping that this time, man would keep himself pure and walk in the ways of God, so that God's plan for their redemption could come to pass.

GOD'S COVENANT WITH NOAH

God also made a covenant with Noah:

> *I will not again curse the ground any more for man's sake; for the imagination of man's heart is evil from his youth; neither will I again smite any more every thing living, as I have done* (Genesis 8:21b).

> *And I, behold, I establish My covenant with you, and with* **your** **seed** *after you....And I will establish My covenant with you; neither shall all flesh be cut off any more by the waters of a flood; neither shall there any more be a flood to destroy the earth. And God said, This is the token of the covenant which I make between Me and you...for perpetual generations: I do set My bow in the cloud, and it shall be for a token of a covenant between Me and the earth* (Genesis 9:9,11-13).

Although satan and his evil companions had been reeling under the blow of the flood upon their handiwork (the giants), this new covenant that God had made with Noah, wherein He promised never to flood the earth again, seemed to reenergize them, for it appeared as if God had trapped Himself with this new promise.

But God's thoughts are higher than satan's thoughts.

Satan decided once more to pollute the seed of man. It had been effective once, so he tried the same method again. Genesis 6:4a tells us:

> *There were giants in the earth in those days* [Noah's day, before the flood]; *and also after that* [after Noah's flood!].

Once more, satan used his cohorts, the fallen angels, to reproduce with the daughters of men, which again resulted in an unholy offspring in the form of *giants*. They occupied the land of Canaan prior to the arrival of Moses.

Satan was determined to corrupt the *pure seed* of God's people, out of which was to come his greatest *foe*!

GOD'S WARNING TO ISRAEL

Throughout the Old Testament, you will find God warning Israel to keep themselves pure and undefiled, for with these giants came their *gods and religions*, the head of whom was satan.

> *When the Lord thy God shall cut off the nations from before thee, whither thou goest to possess them, and thou succeedest them, and dwellest in their land; take heed to thyself that thou be not snared by following them, after that they be destroyed from before thee; and that thou inquire not after their gods, saying, How did these nations serve their gods? even so will I do likewise* (Deuteronomy 12:29-30).

> *If thy brother, the son of thy mother, or thy son, or thy daughter, or the wife of thy bosom, or thy friend, which is as thine own soul, entice thee secretly, saying, let us go and serve other gods, which thou hast not known, thou, nor thy fathers; namely, of the gods of the people which are round about you, nigh unto thee, or far off from thee, from the one end of the earth even unto the other end of the earth; thou shalt not consent unto him, nor hearken unto him; neither shall thine eye pity him, neither shalt thou spare, neither shalt thou conceal him: but thou shalt surely **kill** him* (Deuteronomy 13:6-9a).

GOD'S COVENANT WITH ABRAHAM

God identified the offspring giants of the fallen angels for Abram (Abraham).

> *In the same day the Lord made a covenant with Abram, saying, Unto thy seed have I given this land, from the river of Egypt unto the great river, the river Euphrates:* [the land of] *the Kenites, and the Kenizzites, and the Kedmonites, and the Hittites, and the Perizzites, and the Rephaims, and the Amorites, and the Canaanites, and the Girgashites, and the Jebusites* (Genesis 15:18-21).

All these tribes of peoples lived in the area of Canaan, which was where God intended placing the children of Israel...the land flowing with milk and honey.

> *For mine Angel shall go before thee, and bring thee in unto the Amorites, and the Hittites, and the Perizzites, and the Canaanites, the Hivites, and the Jebusites:* **and I will cut them off**. *Thou shalt not bow down to their gods, nor serve them, nor do after their works: but thou shalt utterly overthrow them, and quite break down their images. ... And I will set thy bounds from the Red sea even unto the sea of the Philistines, and from the desert unto the river: for* **I will deliver** *the inhabitants of the land* **into your hand***; and thou shalt* **drive them out before thee**. *Thou shalt make no covenant* [agreement] *with them, nor with their gods.* **They shall not dwell in thy land**, *lest they make thee sin against Me: for if thou serve their gods, it will surely be a snare unto thee* (Exodus 23:23-24,31-33).

EXODUS

When Moses led the people out of Egypt, they crossed the wilderness and headed towards Canaan. The Lord had already *promised Canaan unto Abraham's seed* and informed them that *He would defeat and give into their hands all the giant nations*. Yet when Moses came to the outskirts of the land of Canaan, he sent a ruler from each tribe to spy out the land, and only two, *Joshua and Caleb*, brought back a good report. All agreed that the land truly was a land flowing with milk and honey—all that the Lord had promised and more. But they said:

> *Nevertheless the people be strong that dwell in the land, and the cities are walled, and very great: and moreover we saw the children of Anak there. The Amalekites dwell in the land of the south: and the Hittites, and the Jebusites, and the Amorites, dwell in the mountains: all the Canaanites dwell by the sea, and by the coast of Jordan. And Caleb stilled the people before Moses, and said, Let us go up at once, and* **possess** *it; for we are well able to overcome it* [Caleb was exercising faith in God's covenant promise to Abraham's seed]. *But the men that went up with him said, We be not able to go up against the people; for they are* **stronger than we**.

> *And they brought up an evil report of the land which they had*
> *searched unto the children of Israel, saying, The land, through*
> *which we have gone to search it, is a land that eateth up the inhab-*
> *itants thereof; and all the people that we saw in it are* **men of a**
> **great stature.** *And there we saw the* **giants,** *the sons of Anak,*
> *which come of the giants* [descendants]: *and we were in our own*
> *sight as grasshoppers, and so we were in their sight* (Numbers
> 13:28-33).

You can imagine how angry God was with them for their lack of faith. He had already agreed to kill all the giant nations for them through His promise to Abraham. Then God wanted to kill all the faithless people, with the exception of Joshua and Caleb. But Moses pleaded with God for their lives. Consequently, because of their unbelief, God refused to let them enter into the promised land and take their rightful inheritance. Instead, He took them on a hike into the wilderness for the next 40 years. Joshua and Caleb were the only two adults of that generation who *did* enter into Canaan territory; the rest perished for their lack of faith.

Joshua became a mighty warrior for the Lord. But have you noticed that throughout his many battles in the land of Canaan, God always gave him the same instructions? He had to *"utterly destroy all that was in the city, both man and woman, young and old..."* (Josh. 6:21). Now, God does not normally make war on women and children, but the *giant seed* was to be wiped out at all costs. God had to eradicate this corruption in order to fulfill His eternal plan and give the world its promised Messiah. All trace of the seed of the fallen angels had to be obliterated.

THE PURE LINEAGE OF THE MESSIAH

To explain the need to annihilate entire nations, we need to move into the New Testament. Please note the first words written are the genealogy of the Messiah! (see Matt. 1:1-17). This is clear evidence that God succeeded in His plan to keep a pure lineage. God fought long and hard and was very longsuffering towards fickle man to maintain a pure wholesome line from which to produce the Messiah,

Jesus Christ. He chose Mary as the vehicle, and Jesus was born into an ordinary working-class family.

Satan had been on the lookout for the promised Redeemer for centuries, fully knowing who the Son of God was, in all His majesty and power in the Heavens. Every angel (of which he had been one, before he received the new name of satan) knew Him to be glorious. The devil was knocked completely off guard when the promised Messiah was born into a lowly family. Gabriel announced to the earth the birth of a "Savior for mankind." Satan was certainly not expecting that the promised Messiah would be born in a stable; it was inconceivable knowing of His majesty in Heaven. He couldn't comprehend that this simple stable could house the long-awaited, promised Messiah. The devil found it hard to comprehend and believe. Nevertheless, satan, through King Herod, had all the Jewish babies less than two years of age murdered, to make sure that if this new baby was indeed the Messiah, he would be killed in the horrific slaughter that followed. But Joseph and Mary were warned and fled with Jesus into Egypt.

Satan kept his eyes on Jesus as the child grew into manhood and became an ordinary carpenter. He kept a constant lookout for the Messiah. He could not comprehend that the Savior would live on earth as a lowly ordinary tradesman.

When John the Baptist baptized Jesus, the devil stood by, as the first public acknowledgment was made of the promised Messiah. After John the Baptist baptized Jesus, God's dove rested on Him, and a voice from Heaven confirmed Jesus' heavenly status. *"This is my beloved Son, in whom I am well pleased"* (Matt. 3:17). Satan was confused. This ordinary carpenter was the Messiah?

Jesus went into the desert, and the devil swiftly followed Him to find out the truth! Notice what question satan repeatedly asked Jesus, *"If Thou be the Son of God..."* (see Matt. 4:1-11, especially verses 3 and 6).

Satan was pretty sure Jesus must have been the Son of God, the Messiah, but was not positive. He found it hard to believe God's Son could have been manifested in such an ordinary human form. He had known Jesus (the Word) in all His glory, majesty, and power, before He came to earth! Knowing the eminence that the Son of God held in the Kingdom of Heaven, he (not having the same sacrificial nature as the Lord) could not comprehend His choice in becoming a simple lowly carpenter, especially when everything that ever existed, belonged to Him! Until the day Jesus hung on the cross at Calvary, satan was still not a hundred percent convinced that Jesus was the Messiah.

When Jesus hung on the cross, satan used the mouth of the mockers and scorners, asking, *"If Thou be the Son of God, come down..."* (Matt. 27:40b). I think that by the time Jesus was dying, His godly magnificence was glaringly obvious even to the unbelievers. The air was charged with emotion, and darkness covered the land. The Light of the world was going out, and even satan had no more doubts as to who Jesus Christ really was!

By then, he realized that something very dangerous to him was taking place. He must have been shaking in his boots, because he knew that at any given time, *if this was the Son of God*, He had only to give the word in the heavenly realm, and myriads of angels would come to His rescue.

> *Thinkest thou that I cannot now pray to My Father, and He shall presently give Me more than twelve legions of angels? But how then shall the Scriptures be fulfilled, that thus it must be?* (Matthew 26:53-54)

Satan gave one more cheap verbal shot at Jesus,

> *If He be the King of Israel, let Him now come down from the cross, and we will believe Him. He trusted in God; let Him deliver Him now, if He will have Him: for He said, I am the Son of God* [satan said through the mouth of one of Christ's tormentors] (Matthew 27:42b-43).

But too late! The ultimate sacrifice was about to take place. Jesus Christ was about to lay down His life to atone for Adam's disobedience and the sins of mankind. Satan was one very worried angel. He now had a change of mind about getting rid of Jesus. Although he originally wanted Jesus killed and out of the way at any cost, he realized another agenda was taking place—God's agenda. So he made a last attempt to prevent Christ from dying on the cross. He now realized, too late, that if Jesus died and obeyed God's plan implicitly to become a sacrifice for mankind's sins, he would legally *buy* back for man the original privileges that were given to Adam and Eve before the fall.

Jesus did go to the cross and His obedience **repurchased** *the earth for mankind.*

Satan thought that he and his human agents had made a public shame of Christ as He hung on the cross; but the cross turned out to be Christ's triumph and the public defeat of satan!

> *And* [Christ] *having spoiled principalities and powers, He made a show of them openly, triumphing over them in it* (Colossians 2:15).

The holy Godhead had become the master of mankind again. Our blessed Lord placed the authority and dominion of this planet Earth once more into the hands of mankind by paying the supreme sacrifice—death.

Once Almighty God had accepted the sacrifice of Jesus, Jesus went down to hell, picked up the keys of death and hell, and preached salvation to all the righteous who had died before Jesus had paid the ultimate sacrifice on the cross. Jesus had been *bruised* on the cross, but satan had been *crushed*!

From that moment, satan had no more official authority over the earth or over any person who accepted the sacrifice of Jesus Christ, making Him their personal Savior. *"The earth is the Lord's, and the fullness thereof"* (Ps. 24:1a). However, the *unbelievers*, who obey *satan* rather than God, still give satan a legal right to stay here on planet Earth until the day that Jesus comes back again in triumph to sit on His throne here on earth.

Satan is *no longer the legal ruler of the planet Earth*. Rather, Jesus Christ and through Him all the believers, should be the true present-day rulers of this planet!

Since then, Jesus Christ has spent over 2000 years uniting a Body of believers together—believers who love and worship God with all their soul, spirit, and body. They do not serve other gods...or do they? Yes, God is still trying to prevent His children from going after *other gods*.

Now that you understand the enormous battle that God had to fight in order to keep sinful mankind pure, are you going to continue to play with the toys satan holds out for you? Or will you, like Joshua of old, become a mighty warrior for the Lord and part of the last-days, glorious army?

The Messiah has now been; therefore, satan is reserving his forces for the last stand at the second coming of Christ. There is no longer any need to pollute the "seed of women"—the Messiah has already been. But the devil knows the Scriptures well and also knows what his end will be; so what has he to lose? He has set himself the task of taking as many of God's creation with him to his final abode—*hell*.

How does he put his plan into action? By causing mankind to walk in sin, deception, and unbelief. How does he do this? His ways are numerous, and we will learn about them in the following chapters.

5

OUR WEAPONS

When Jesus left us with the command, *"Go ye into all the world..."* (see Mark 16:15-18), and *"As My Father hath sent Me, even so send I you"* (John 20:21b), there was no way as our Commander that *He forgot to give us the ability, power, and weaponry needed to combat the enemy.*

Our first weapon is the power in the *name of Jesus*. Jesus told us to use it to defeat the devil. When we use it, it has all the authority just the same as if Jesus was using it.

The power is the *name of Jesus*—that is the *warhead*. The "instrument" that carries the *power* is called the *Holy Spirit*—the dumonis—*dynamite*; and *faith* pulls the *trigger*! And we, His army, need these weapons to maim, kill, and remove the enemy.

No force on earth, under the earth, or above the earth can overcome this power...apart from God Himself.

You have a mandate and authority from Heaven to use the *name of Jesus*. You might not feel as if you have any power; but remember the sun's rays have power even though they cannot be seen. You don't feel, see, or touch this power; but in faith, *you speak it.*

To the layman, this may sound foolish; but Christ Himself said, "*And whatsoever ye shall ask **in My name**, that will I do, that the Father may be glorified in the Son...*" (John 14:13). We don't have to beg for anything, or plead; we simply ask in *Jesus' name*, and He is only too willing to bring it to pass to glorify the Father.

When Peter and John saw the lame beggar at the gate who asked for alms, the disciples didn't fish in their pockets for small change. Nor did they quote Scripture, telling him that he should be living in prosperity and health according to God's Word...then walk away. No, they went straight to the heart of the matter.

"*Then Peter said, Silver and gold have I none; but such as I have give I thee: **In the name of Jesus Christ of Nazareth** rise up and walk*" (Acts 3:6). And the beggar did walk. In fact, he jumped and leapt. The people inside the temple knew this beggar of old, and were amazed that he could now walk. So, Peter took the opportunity to explain about Jesus. "***And His name** through faith in **His name** hath made this man strong, whom ye see and know*" (Acts 3:16a).

The apostle Paul also knew where the power lay. A young woman who had joined herself to his party as it traveled through the town, was possessed of an evil spirit of divination and led people to believe she was part of Paul's entourage. It bothered Paul, because he did not want people to be deceived by her, and after several days, Paul had had enough. "*And this did she many days. But Paul, being grieved, turned and said to the spirit* [controlling her], *I command thee in the name of Jesus Christ to come out of her. And he* [the spirit] *came out the same hour*" (Acts 16:18).

All the disciples did and said was in the *name of Jesus Christ*, and many miracles and healings took place.

> And whatsoever ye do in word or deed, do all **in the name** of the Lord Jesus, giving thanks to God and the Father by Him (Colossians 3:17).

You might ask, "How can a name hold so much power?"

> For unto us a child is born, unto us a Son is given: and the government shall be upon His shoulder: and His **name** shall be called

Wonderful, Counsellor, The mighty God, The everlasting Father, The Prince of Peace (Isaiah 9:6).

*And Jesus came and spake unto them, saying, **All power** is given unto Me in heaven and in earth* (Matthew 28:18).

*Wherefore God also hath highly exalted Him, and given Him a **name** which is **above every name**: that at the **name of Jesus** every knee should bow, of things in heaven, and things in earth, and things under the earth* (Philippians 2:9-10).

*And Jesus came and spake unto them, saying, **All power** is given unto Me in heaven and in earth* (Matthew 28:18).

Jesus Christ, and His name, have authority in three realms!

*And what is the exceeding greatness of His power to us-ward who believe, according to the working of His mighty power, which He wrought in Christ, when He raised Him from the dead, and set Him at His own right hand in the heavenly places, far above all principality, and power, and might, and dominion, and **every name that is named**, not only in this world, but also in that which is to come: and hath put all things under His feet, and gave Him to be the head over all things to the church* (Ephesians 1:19-22).

His name demands response in every realm. The amazing thing is that He has ordered us, the believers, to use His name.

*…Verily, verily, I say unto you, **Whatsoever** ye shall ask the Father **in My name**, He will give it you. Hitherto have ye asked nothing **in My name**: ask, and ye shall receive, that your joy may be full* (John 16:23-24).

*And these signs shall follow them that believe; **In My name** shall they cast out devils; they shall speak with new tongues; they shall take up serpents; and if they drink any deadly thing, it shall not hurt them; they shall lay hands on the sick, and they shall recover* (Mark 16:17-18).

Your personality or ability will not get the job done; it is the *name of Jesus* that has the *power*.

Power to set free.

Power to become sons (see John 1:12).

Power to save (see John 20:31).

Power to forgive sins (see Luke 24:47).

Power to heal (see Acts 3:6,16).

Power to answer prayer (see John 14:13).

Power to deliver from evil spirits (see Acts 16:18).

If you cannot grasp that behind the *name of Jesus Christ* stands all of Heaven to make sure a request or command is carried out, and that we the believers have *every right to use it*, then you will be a *powerless* believer. You won't be seeing many answers to prayer or miracles.

Have you ever come to an intersection and standing in the center of the road is a policeman directing traffic? When the officer raises his hand to halt a car, it stops! But if that car chooses to continue, it could hit the officer and do great damage to him, wherein it would be realized that the officer's puny hand was no match for the car's power. However, when a driver sees that officer with his hand raised showing him to halt, he knows that *behind* that puny hand stands the whole police force, the army, and the government of that land, to enforce that authority!

Now, that puny hand is what it is like in Heaven when a saint uses the *name of Jesus*. All of Heaven enforces that authority—in three realms!

Once you realize the *power* behind the *name*, as is found in Philippians 2:9-11, you understand that every being in this world, in Heaven, and under the earth, has to bow the knee in obedience to Jesus Christ. And because He has given us *"power of attorney"* (authorized permission) to use His name, all in Heaven and earth and under the earth have to obey our commands when we use the *name of Jesus Christ*, just the same as if Jesus Christ Himself had given them. Once you can understand this, your Christian walk will be far more dynamic!

OUR WEAPON

Our weapon is the same one that Jesus used. Whenever satan confronted Jesus, Jesus simply quoted from the Word of God to defeat him. It worked for Jesus, and it works for the saints.

> *Then was Jesus led up of the Spirit into the wilderness to be tempted by the devil. And when He had fasted forty days and forty nights, He was afterward an hungered. And when the tempter came to Him, he said, If Thou be the Son of God, command that these stones be made bread. But He answered and **said, It is written**, Man shall not live by bread alone, but by every word that proceedeth out of the mouth of God. Then the devil taketh Him up into the holy city, and setteth Him on a pinnacle of the temple, and saith unto Him, If Thou be the Son of God, cast Thyself down: for it is written, He shall give His angels charge concerning Thee: and in their hands they shall bear Thee up, lest at any time Thou dash Thy foot against a stone. Jesus **said** unto him, **It is written** again, Thou shalt not tempt the Lord thy God. Again, the devil taketh Him up into an exceeding high mountain, and showeth Him all the kingdoms of the world, and the glory of them; and saith unto Him, All these things will I give Thee, if Thou wilt fall down and worship me. Then **saith** Jesus unto him, Get thee hence, satan: for **it is written**, Thou shalt worship the Lord thy God, and Him only shalt thou serve. Then the devil leaveth Him, and, behold, angels came and ministered unto Him* (Matthew 4:1-11).

God's Word is law. It is the weapon Jesus used to defeat His enemy, the devil, and it is just as powerful today to defeat our enemy. God's Word in the believer's mouth is as powerful as God's Word in Christ's mouth.

6

SATAN ATTACKS IN THREE WAYS

Satan attacks in three ways:

1. By oppression.

2. By possession.

3. By a direct attack upon a person's spirit.

Demon possession and demon oppression are very different. For example:

> ...they brought unto Him all sick people that were taken with divers diseases and torments, and those which were **possessed** with devils, and those which were lunatic, and those that had the palsy; and He healed them (Matthew 4:24).

Here the people were "*possessed*" with devils. The definition of *possessed* in the dictionary, means, "to own, to have control of, to seize or to enter into and influence."

Matthew 16:15-16 states:

He saith unto them, But whom say ye that I am? And Simon Peter answered and said, Thou art the Christ, the Son of the living God.

Peter recognized Jesus as *"Christ, the Son of the living God,"* and Jesus acknowledged that flesh and blood had not revealed that piece of information to Peter. This portion of Scripture explains that Peter had accepted Jesus as the Son of God, which would make Peter *a believer*. Yet just three verses later, notice what Peter said when Jesus told the disciples that He must go to Jerusalem to suffer and die.

Then Peter took Him, and began to rebuke Him, saying, Be it far from Thee, Lord: this shall not be unto Thee. But He turned, and said unto Peter, Get thee behind Me, satan: thou art an offence unto Me: for thou savourest not the things that be of God, but those that be of men (Matthew 16:22-23).

Peter was *not possessed* of a demon, one that had full control of him, but was simply oppressed by one. He had listened to the voice of satan whispering in his ear, telling him that Jesus should not go to the cross. That is called *oppression*—an *outside influence* working on Peter. Jesus recognized it and spoke directly to the devil. We all would have no hope today if Jesus had listened to Peter, and not recognized satan's cheap attempt at preventing Him from redeeming mankind on the cross.

A *direct attack upon the spirit* of man by satan is usually caused by using one believer to attack another. This thrust by the devil serves to undermine a saint's *standing* in Christ. An unbeliever's attack upon a believer does not offend the believer as he expects the unbeliever to misunderstand a Christian's beliefs. But when one *believer* questions another *believer's* beliefs, it knocks him completely off balance.

For example, he might be told that *"whatever he receives from the Bible—his interpretation—is twisted and not from God."* The believer might lose confidence in interpreting Scripture, which causes him to doubt that he can receive comfort or solace from the Bible—the mainstay of his belief. The Word of God has been shaken for him, and he can't trust himself to read or understand it properly. Satan's purpose in this kind of attack is to completely cripple him spiritually. But God is faithful and sticks very close to him at this time. Christians should be on the alert for this kind of attack. A good talk with their pastor or a spiritual leader can soon clear up any misunderstanding and help them to stay on track in their Christian theology.

A Christian cannot be demon possessed, but he can be oppressed.

Man is a tripartite being, made up of *spirit, soul*, and *body*. A believer can have a demon operating in his *body* (sickness), and even in the *soulish* area (mind). But if Jesus Christ dwells in his *spirit*, then it is impossible for satan to dwell there too and possess him. No matter how oppressed a believer is, his spirit can resist and his body can be released from evil spirits, as long as he is willing to accept deliverance from them.

God is gentle with new converts, and throughout their Christian walk, He will continue to show them the areas in their lives that need to be cleaned up by the Holy Spirit. For instance, a spirit of sarcasm might start to manifest itself over and over again in someone's life. At this time, that person can't avoid realizing that as a Christian he should not be speaking that way. He should accept that the Lord is exposing an area in his life that needs cleaning up. He needs to repent before the Lord and get rid of the sarcasm by getting someone to help if he can't do the deliverance himself. Often, just when someone is feeling pleased that he has been released from sarcasm, the Lord will pinpoint some other area in his life that also needs cleaned up. And so it continues until his body becomes completely clean of all evil influences.

It's important to remember that while he is being cleaned up, so are his brothers and sisters in the Lord. Becoming a believer does not immediately cause one to be "Christ-like" and perfect. Each believer is a *"work in progress."* So, apply the following Scripture: *"Love covers over a multitude of sins"* (1 Pet. 4:8). If things don't look right, be patient, because like yourself, other believers are also in the process of being perfected by God. Pray for them instead of judging them.

Sometimes, when a believer backslides or starts to sink into deep waters, it is because the Lord is showing him a part of himself that he does not want to see, or a part of himself that he cannot accept. And sometimes he rebels and starts to pull away from the Lord. This can become a chronic situation. However, God will not, nor cannot, change *His* mind on the matter. If He spots sin in a believer's life, it cannot stay there; for no sin is acceptable in Heaven. And if God will not or cannot change His mind, that means the saint will eventually have to change *his*. So, he will go one more lap around the mountain until he accepts what the Lord is showing him about himself. God demands he face the problem squarely, and acknowledge before Him that he does not want the problem operating in his life anymore. Then he should wait upon the Lord to see what He wants the believer to do, and then do it immediately. If he continues to resist God, he can only harm himself. God will bring him back time and again until he faces the problem and overcomes it.

HOW DEMONS MAKE THEIR ENTRY

No believer would willingly retreat if satan made a direct attack upon him. He would stand his ground, grit his teeth, take up his faith shield, and engage in battle with the "Word of God." Satan knows this, so he rarely tries a frontal attack. He is still just as devious as he was in the Garden of Eden, subtle and sneaky; and his minions, the evil spirits, have the same nature.

An evil spirit's purpose is to hassle and torment a person, working together with other spirits to entangle a person to the point that a *strongman* can enter his body.

Satan knows that even a baby Christian has the ability to inflict deep wounds on him with the Word of God. So, he prefers to come at a person indirectly and in small insignificant ways to start with, slowly building up to the crunch when a man's life is in such a tangle that he is rendered useless to the Lord. And nearly every time it works! Believers are on the lookout for the direct attacks, but are not so aware of the subtle ways the devil enmeshes them in a situation whereby they give him legal right to take a thrust at them.

Let's study a simple scenario of how the enemy can operate. He has carte blanche to operate in the lives of unbelievers, but sometimes believers let themselves get entangled too!

Someone might say or do something to another person, who is then offended and feels *hurt*. Satan works on these feelings, and the person starts to feel *resentment* towards the one who hurt him. He loses his joy and starts to avoid places where he knows the one who hurt him often frequents. Day and night the hurt plays over and over in his mind, and each time it gets a little larger than it actually was to begin with. A *spirit of pride* then starts to pressure him, and everything the one who has hurt him says or does is magnified out of proportion so that he starts to declare into the situation far more than there originally was.

By this time the Holy Spirit is probably shouting, "Forgive, forgive!" but if he hardens his heart, watch out! Doing it God's way, using forgiveness, protects him. Doing it the world's way, getting even, leaves him wide open to evil influences.

If the offended one is not prepared to fall on his face before God and ask His forgiveness, he is in real trouble. He certainly needs to ask the person who offended him to forgive his attitude *towards him*. This action is very necessary, or he leaves himself open to spirits of delusion, strife, confusion, deceit, and self-pity, to name just a few; and his heart is hardened towards the godly solution.

He becomes unteachable to advice, justified in his own eyes, and misunderstood by everyone else...and wide open to receive *the spirit of rebellion*.

An immature believer might not be too quick to forgive the one who offended him, afraid he will be presumed an easy target...next time! By now, the person's attitude is really showing, and he starts to justify himself to the people around him, so that they *know* how much the offender has hurt him.

He cannot speak that person's name without his true feelings coming through his voice. And it develops until his mouth and actions start to show *bitterness*. Romans 3:13,18 (NIV) says:

> *Their throats are open graves; their tongues practice deceit. The poison of vipers is on their lips....There is no fear of God before their eyes* [for the cursing and destruction of their mouths, nor for the nonfulfillment of the commandment of Jesus to *love* one another; see also John 15:12,17; 1 Pet. 1:22].

The Bible goes even further:

If a man say, I love God, and hateth his brother, he is a liar: for he that loveth not his brother whom he hath seen, how can he love God whom he hath not seen? And this commandment have we from Him, That he who loveth God love his brother also (1 John 4:20-21).

By the time the situation has gone this far—being *hurt*, feeling *resentment*, harboring *unforgiveness*—the *spirit of bitterness* then tries to take root in him. Satan and his demons, whose aim it is to try to get this strongman established in his spirit, have orchestrated all these "feelings."

If at this stage he still refuses to forgive, then he has a definite problem.

Anyone who hates [abominates, detests] his brother [in Christ] is [at heart] a murderer, and you know that no murderer has eternal life abiding [preserving] within him (1 John 3:15 AMP).

A believer should conduct his life according to God's Word, operating in forgiveness and reconciliation; however, the unbeliever unknowingly falls into the trap satan orchestrates for him.

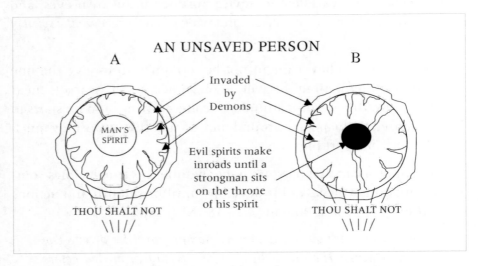

The unbeliever's defense is his own self-will. His *willingness* to sin makes inroads into his spirit.

When the Gospel is rejected, the cracks and fissures in a man's spirit, i.e. *lust, greed, hatred, anger, rebellion, etc.* make *greater and greater inroads* into his spirit. An unbeliever is ignorantly unaware of this and quite happy to live that way, thus becoming deeper and deeper enmeshed with these spirits. Eventually, oppression by these spirits can give way to *possession* by these evil spirits.

The willingness to sin stifles the godly commands that have been written on *every* man's heart. The unbeliever pushes *away* the laws of God and so hardens his heart, so that he no longer hears them anymore.

> *Be not deceived; God is not mocked: for whatsoever a man soweth, that shall he also reap. For he that soweth to his flesh shall of the flesh reap corruption* (Galatians 6:7-8a).

> *For the wages of sin is death; but the gift of God is eternal life through Jesus Christ our Lord* (Romans 6:23).

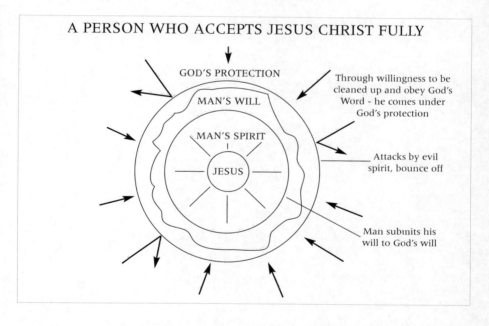

When the enemy shall come in like a flood, the spirit of the Lord shall lift up a standard against him (Isaiah 59:19b).

From the Word of God, believers have knowledge of right and wrong. If the believer chooses to "do it God's way" by putting his will under God's will, then the attacks from satan must bounce off the shield (standard) provided by God.

7

GOD'S ARMOR

Once you accept Christ as your Savior, you become part of God's army; at the same time you are automatically issued with both weapons and armor. The choice to use them is up to you.

> *The night is far spent, the day is at hand: let us therefore cast off the works of darkness, and let us put on the **armor of light** (Romans 13:12).*

> **Put on the whole armor of God**, *that ye may be able to stand against the wiles of the devil (Ephesians 6:11).*

> *For the weapons of our warfare are not carnal, but mighty through God to the pulling down of strongholds (2 Corinthians 10:4).*

What does the armor consist of?

> *And take the **helmet of salvation**, and the **sword of the Spirit**, which is the word of God (Ephesians 6:17).*

> *Stand therefore, having your **loins girt about with truth**, and having on **the breastplate of righteousness**; and **your feet shod with the preparation of the gospel of peace**; above all, taking the*

81

shield of faith; wherewith ye shall be able to quench all the fiery darts of the wicked (Ephesians 6:14-16).

There are many teachings on this subject, and you are free to choose which seems right to you. For myself, I have had two experiences that give me a pretty clear indication as to what the *"armor of God"* really is.

I was six months old in the Lord, and before retiring one night, I had been searching the Scriptures for a certain verse but couldn't find it. During the night, the Lord clearly gave me the verse I had been looking for. When I muttered a sleepy "Thanks, Lord," I suddenly realized to whom I had spoken. I sat up in bed and switched on the side lamp. I looked up the Scripture that I had been given, and as you might guess, it was the very one that I had been looking for. (I was fully awake at this time; *I was not dreaming.*)

I switched off the side lamp and prepared to sleep again, but in the dark, on the wall opposite my bed, there appeared what seemed to be a film, like an old-fashioned home movie. I could see a tall, dense privet hedge and a door in the middle of this hedge. The picture seemed to zoom in onto the door. Suddenly, I was standing in front of the door in the hedge. I then reached out and pushed it open.

Then it became a little jumbled, as if I was being processed or something similar, for abruptly I was inside the door, standing in bright sunlight. I seemed to be in the countryside somewhere.

When I looked down at myself, I was surprised to see myself dressed in what looked like old Roman armor, complete with a helmet and sword in my hand. I stood there not quite knowing what to do, when I become conscious that in a clearing ahead of me were other similarly dressed individuals, just standing or sitting around. I walked towards them. The sun beat down and made me very hot inside the armor.

Some people were sitting down, and some of them had removed pieces of their armor. Some had removed their shoes; others had put down their swords and shields. Still others, feeling the heat, had taken off their short skirts and molded breastplates. They all seemed relaxed sitting there, not doing or saying much, having no purpose or direction. I felt an urgency to keep walking, and no one took any notice of me as I passed through their midst.

On the other side of the clearing was what looked like an old country lane, deeply rutted, as if eroded by the constant passing of a cart or feet. Grass formed a little mound between the two deep ruts. On the right side of the lane was a very dense, high privet hedge that I could not see over or through. On the other side was grassland, leading down to what seemed like a very wide six-lane motorway.

As I started to walk down the rutted lane, noise penetrated my thinking. On my left, on the six-lane motorway, was what appeared to be the happiest group of people. They were laughing and calling to one another, with children joyfully dancing among and around the adults. They were all going in the same direction, walking down the wide motorway, and they were heading in the same direction as I was.

I felt a little isolated as I walked alone on the country lane on the side of the mountain. Deep inside me something responded. As I looked at all the cheerful people, a part of me wanted to join them. But instead, I continued on the rutted roadway, which started to rise steeply in front of me so that I began to walk uphill. Still, my eyes kept straying to the happy bunch of people on the left.

My armor felt heavy and a little uncomfortable at first, but as I got into a steady rhythm of walking, it seemed a little easier to carry.

I walked for some time, ever uphill, and came to a bend in the road. As I came around the bend, I saw that the road proceeded down sharply into a deep valley in front of me. I looked down into the valley and saw that the sun did not penetrate down into the bottom of it. It was dark, and my road seemed to disappear into the murky blackness. I had a foreboding that something hostile was waiting for me down there. Looking across the valley, I could see that the country lane on the other side of the valley rose up again out of the darkness; it was bathed in bright sunlight. The far lane seemed even higher than the part on which I was standing. But I knew that in order to get to the other side, I would not be able to avoid the dark valley in front of me.

I took a deep breath and started to run downhill. As I picked up momentum and ran into the swirling mist in the depths of the valley, missiles of all kinds flew at me. Spears, stones, and arrows hurled at me. I lifted my shield to protect myself, running with it raised above my head. I never saw who was throwing these missiles at me; I just ran like I'd never run before in my life. Abruptly, I broke into the bright sunlight on the other side of the valley, and felt within my breast such an exhilarating surge...I'd made it! By the time I reached the top of the rise in the road on the other side, I was belly laughing!

As I looked behind me into the abyss-like valley, my eyes caught sight of the people on the motorway to the left, which now, because of my ascent, seemed much further below my road. The people appeared to be frenzied and rushing about even more than before; and although there was still laughter, it seemed to be forced as if they were not having as much fun as before.

I turned back towards my rutted road and started to walk again. I was then surprised to see a soldier, dressed in armor like mine and sitting down at the side of the road. I had the impression that he had experienced such a fright going through the valley, that it had paralyzed him. He simply sat. He couldn't go back through the valley, and yet he was afraid to proceed forward. (Some believers are like that when a problem has to be faced in the spiritual realm.)

The road straightened out in front of me but continued to rise steadily. The hedge on my right was still very tall and too thick to see through, but as the lane continued to rise, I now had a clear view of the six-lane motorway on my left, above the tall grass of the fields that separated me from it. Far below me, people were still traveling along, and they seemed even more frenzied in their actions, like trapped rats. Again, they didn't seem to be enjoying their trip as much as they had before. Then I noticed that there were small signposts on my road. One read, "IF YOU WANT A DRINK, COME THIS WAY"; and a small arrow pointed down a tiny dirt path winding through the tall grass to join the motorway far below. Other signs declared, "IF YOU WANT TO GAMBLE...UNLAWFUL SEX...MURDER...." All signs pointed in the same direction—towards the freeway.

I could not see on the motorway side, but I knew there were signposts on the motorway pointing to this top road. "DO YOU WANT

YOUR SINS FORGIVEN? DO YOU NEED JESUS, THE SAVIOR? DO YOU WANT ETERNAL LIFE?"

As I looked down upon the masses of people far below on the motorway still trying desperately to derive some pleasure out of life, I realized why they were so agitated and no longer happy—things of the world had failed to fulfill them. At that moment, there was no longer any pull or desire within me to join them.

I had been climbing steadily and steeply on my lane and suddenly came upon a second valley. This time it was even deeper and darker than before. Its ominous black depths palpitated with evil, but there was no longer any fear in me that I might be harmed. I knew missiles would be fired at me again; I even expected them. Without hesitation, I lifted my shield high, and shouting as if in defiance, like a war cry, I ran down through the valley at top speed, dodging all arrows and missiles, and continued straight up the other side to an even higher level rutted lane. I was so excited when I broke into the sunshine after exiting the valley, that I hopped from foot to foot laughing uncontrollably.

There was a lightness within me, a spring in my step, and my armor no longer felt heavy. As the lane leveled out, I turned at another bend in the road, and I could see very far into the distance. All of a sudden, I observed what seemed to be an endless, great Golden City bathed in the brightest of light. This light seemed to radiate from it and not onto it, as it shimmered in its majestic glory.

I could see an odd soldier in the distance in front of me, identically dressed as me, walking along the long road towards the city. Other soldiers were walking in the same direction. The high hedge on my right had disappeared, and there was a solitary figure, dressed in white, coming from the City towards us. In the distance, I could see that He was stopping at each soldier, embracing each one, and then pointing behind Him towards the Golden City. My spirit knew exactly who He was, and I watched intently as He came closer and closer to me. My heart rejoiced in anticipation of His presence.

He was not handsome, as the world defines it, but He had a beautiful attractiveness about Him. His hair was dark with hints of auburn d cut to just below his ears. He wore a white tunic to calf-length, and He was barefoot...it was Jesus.

He stood right next to me and wrapped His arms around me saying, "Well done," and in that moment, the feeling that came over me was indescribable. Every yearning, every need, every desire was fulfilled and satisfied in that embrace. I seemed to fall into overwhelming love, and an extraordinary peace came over me. I remember a thought crossed through my mind as I looked down at the hair on His calf, which showed up the alabaster white of His feet. He was not as I had imagined Him to be; there were no nail marks on either of His hands or His feet! (This perplexed me until I asked the Lord afterwards to explain why there were no wounds. I was told simply that none of the devil's handiwork would have a final place in Heaven, for Jesus had taken His place on the right hand of the Father).

After the wonderful embrace, Jesus pointed to the City in front of me and said, "Go. Your mansion awaits you." He started to walk on then, and not wanting to part from Him, I asked if I could go with Him. He turned back to face me. He never spoke a word, but answered me by His Spirit directly to my spirit, and I knew it was all right to follow Him. I turned around to retrace my footsteps on the rutted country lane, but on this return trip there were no bends in the road or deep valleys.

We walked for a while, and Jesus greeted more soldiers. But soon, we came into the original clearing that I had first seen after I had entered the door in the hedge.

There were soldiers still there in different stages of undress. They too seemed to know who the person was coming towards them, and they all stood up and called out, "Lord, Lord, Lord!"

But Jesus looked at them and said, "Depart from Me!"

Then I was immediately back in my own bed, but the Lord was still taking to me. I asked, "Lord, why did You turn away from them?"

He answered in His own way. People are born again through salvation; some accept a Savior only to escape hell. Others like the soldier on the road who wouldn't move after he had met opposition in the valley, find the cost of being a believer (living and approaching life by

God's rules and standards) too high. When they feel it is too hard to do it God's way, they start taking off vital pieces of armor. *By their own choice*, they remove their *loincloth of truth* when they speak lies; their *shoes of peace* feel uncomfortable, and they lose their testimony as they slip them off; or they take off their *breastplate* and consequently their *righteousness* vanishes. Situations or circumstances become "too hot for them under the sun" (and satan's hand), so they put down their *shield of faith* and *sword of the Spirit*; those pieces become too heavy a burden to use. Ultimately, of course, they finish up by taking off their *helmets of salvation*.

I believe that we are given our *armor*, but if we don't *maintain* it, we can lose it! Just like Moses' sister Miriam, one can have one's name taken *out* of the Book of Life. Everyone has a duty to follow, and everyone must obey the commands of God...or bear the consequences. God cannot make you truthful, or righteous, or a man of faith; these traits are a way of life that must be chosen *by you*.

Some believers think that because God supplies the armor, it is not necessary to keep putting it on, yet Ephesians 6:11 tells us specifically to *put on* the armor as part of our warfare against the devil. By putting it on each day, you constantly check that every part of your armor is in place; it's a good habit to cultivate.

ANGELIC VISITATION

On the second occasion that the Lord spoke to me about my armor, I had been going through a difficult time, experiencing a full barrage of attacks from the devil on a daily basis.

Dawn was just breaking, and I was sleeping alone in the bedroom when I was suddenly conscious of not being alone anymore. I turned, and there at the side of my bed was the most beautiful angel. He was very tall with ear-length, golden, curly hair. He was dressed in the same old Roman-type armor that I had seen before, except he wore no helmet. And he had two of the most beautiful huge wings; each glowed with a dazzling whiteness. Each soft feather in the wings was exquisitely perfect and in flawless formation. I somehow knew he was my *personal angel*.

He spoke my name softly, and then told me to remember to *put on my armor each day*. And although I never left the bed, I saw myself in my nightclothes on my knees at the side of the bed, and I heard myself say, *"I put on the breastplate of righteousness, the loincloth of truth, the shoes of peace, the helmet of salvation, the shield of faith, and the sword of the Spirit."* And as I spoke each item of armor, the armor was actually forming on my body, so that when I stood up beside the bed, I was dressed in full armor. It was the same as the angel's armor, except that I had on a *helmet of salvation*, and he didn't.

The angel spoke again as he pointed to my armor. "When you put on your armor, you look just like that in the spirit world, so put it on every day."

Now, if God thought it so important to send an angel down to warn me to put my armor on, on a daily basis, I would be a fool not to do it. God has supplied believers with a full set of armor for a reason, so make a daily checklist and ensure that every piece is in place.

The marvelous thing about everyone wearing the same armor is that the devil is never sure who is inside it; he can't see the face inside the helmet. He can't tell who is inside the armor. It could even be Jesus...and satan doesn't want to tangle with Him!

> *Put on the whole armor of God, that ye may be able to stand against the wiles of the devil. For we wrestle not against flesh and blood, but against principalities, against powers, against the rulers of the darkness of this world, against spiritual wickedness in high places. Wherefore take unto you the whole armor of God, that ye may be able to withstand in the evil day, and having done all, to stand. Stand therefore, having your loins girt about with truth, and having on the breastplate of righteousness; and your feet shod with the preparation of the gospel of peace; above all, taking the shield of faith, wherewith ye shall be able to quench all the fiery darts of the wicked, and take the helmet of salvation, and the sword of the Spirit, which is the word of God: praying always with all prayer and supplication in the Spirit, and watching thereunto with all perseverance and supplication for all saints (Ephesians 6:11-18).*

8

ARE ANGELS AND EVIL SPIRITS THE SAME THING?

There are two entirely different words used for these entities.

Angels are ἀγγέλον and evil spirits are ἀκάθαρτων in the original Greek language.

Satan is σατανα, (a fallen angel), adversary, false accuser, and slanderer (see 1 Tim. 3:11; 2 Tim. 3:3; Titus 2:3). Satan is known as the prince of demons. There is only one prince, but many demons. He also has an angelic body and cannot enter bodily into anyone. His name is σατανα or, in the Greek, *diabŏlŏs*[1].

Angels *have bodies with bodily parts*—hands, feet, eyes, faces, and other parts, as already discussed in Chapter Three. Therefore, they cannot enter bodily into another being.

Diamonion and *Diamon*[2] are evil spirits, used 76 times in the Bible. These are *disembodied* spirits, which cannot operate *without a body to work through*. They can enter in and out of bodies freely, with their host's permission. They are also called devils (see Mark 16:17); familiar spirits (see Lev. 20:6); unclean spirits (see Mark 1:27); evil spirits (see Luke 7:21); and seducing spirits (see 1 Tim. 4:1).

So where do demons come from if they are not angels?

Let's look at angels or more specifically "fallen angels" first, to confirm they are not demons. We know some angels did not keep their first estate, or to their own principality. They did not remain in their own realm, but left it and entered into the "human realm" of earth. They devised the plan to corrupt the seed of the daughters of men by having sexual relations with them and producing *giants*. So, these angels lived contrary to the original, designated, God-ordained plan for them...by corrupting mankind (see Gen. 6:4). The sins they committed went far beyond that of falling from grace, by rebelling with lucifer. *They are now confined to hell* for this sin (see Jude 1:6).

The question is: If all fallen angels have already been confined to hell, then who will be left to fight with the devil against God in the middle of Daniel's 70th week, before the second coming of Jesus Christ?

There are those that have already been confined to hell (a portion of the original outcasts with lucifer), who tried to *corrupt the seed of mankind* and are awaiting God's judgment. And the second lot are those who rebelled with lucifer, but are not yet in hell. All the good angels that minister to God are with Him in Heaven, and it seems that all the other angels can be accounted for.

That still leaves us with the problem of where *did* the demons come from if evil spirits are not angels fallen from grace?

DEMONS COME FROM...

When lucifer was originally given the first brand-new earth to prepare for God's masterpiece—mankind, angels were allocated to him to help oversee the preparations for completing the planet Earth. Angels themselves are messengers and overseers, not laborers, so God provided some laborers in the form of spirits, who did the actual work.

God's heavenly inhabitants are not confined to merely angels, or devils, as we know them; as discussed in previous chapters, there are several types of spiritual beings. We are very limited in our knowledge of the extent of heavenly beings—both good and bad, but *"these are they whom the Lord hath sent to walk to and fro through the earth"* (Zech. 1:10b).

I believe that at the time that lucifer prepared the earth and was corrupting the angels who went along with his rebellion, some of these "labor" spirit beings heard and knew what was going on. It is also my opinion that not all these spirit beings went along with lucifer's rebellion and slander—and our just God would have rescued them at the appropriate time. However, those who went along with lucifer in the trafficking of slander and rebellion, got caught up in the ensuing battle between lucifer and God. Consequently, God cut off lucifer and cast him and the one third of the angels that rebelled out of Heaven. Obviously, although unsaid, any other spirits beings that were in rebellion would have been thrown out too.

The story of the revenge of lucifer and the fallen angels is well documented, but what about the spirit beings that joined forces with lucifer and were still on earth when God obliterated it and made it void? They couldn't go back to Heaven, and lucifer had no further use for them at that time. I believe they hung around and hovered over the first flooded earth for the longest time until God re-created the second earth (see Gen. 1:3) and until lucifer devised a plan to regain control of the earth.

It was at that time that satan remembered these spirit beings; and when he set up the hierarchy of his kingdom, he had a use for them once more. He would use these evil spirits and demons to torment the precious mankind whom God had created.

To summarize, angels have bodies of their own and cannot enter into human bodies. Whereas, evil spirits/demons have no bodies, and in fact, need a human host or animal body to be able to operate. Study again the chart in Chapter Three of satan's kingdom structure.

DON'T GO LOOKING FOR DEVILS UNDER EVERY BUSH!

Have you ever heard the expression, "Don't go looking for devils under every bush"? I heard it at a church meeting recently, and as the speaker continued to preach, the Lord cut right across my thought realm and said, *"And that is the most erroneous statement made today!"*

In a flash, the Lord showed me the Selous Scout Regiment of former Rhodesia in Central Africa. Near the end of the war, soldiers were on duty for one month and off duty one month, on a month, off a month. The Lord continued, *"Do you think that even on the occasions that the soldiers were "off duty" from the war front, their training did not operate automatically and they were not naturally on the alert for terrorists?"*

On the contrary, I knew these troops were alert, and their suspicions and promptness saved many lives from what could have been horrific accidents caused by bombs planted in the very towns in which they lived. They expected to meet the enemy on the battlefront; but in their own hometowns, they should have been able to relax, and not look for terrorists under every bush! But thank God, that while they might have been off duty, they were never unalert.

Casting out evil spirits was an important part of the ministry of Jesus Christ too—a third of it, in fact; and in order to have a balanced ministry, it is important that we possess the ability to do the same. We must be fully aware of the spirit world, especially if we are going to belong to a glorious *army* for Jesus Christ on His return.

Consider all the Books that the apostle Paul wrote in the New Testament and all the Books written by the other apostles under the unction of the Holy Spirit, yet not once did they find it necessary to warn believers "not to look under every bush for devils!" Because this statement has been preached in the church for so long, many saints do not do anything at all about the devil, or at best, leave it to the known experts and pastors.

But to do nothing is not in line with the Word of God. Jesus gave a commission to His Church:

> *And He ordained twelve, that they should be with Him, and that He might send them forth to preach, and to have power to heal sicknesses, and to cast out devils* (Mark 3:14-15).

> *And when He called unto Him His twelve disciples He gave them power against unclean spirits, to cast them out, and to heal all manner of disease* (Matthew 10:1).

"Ah," you say, "that was only for the early disciples." Considering that the Bible says that God has no favorites, are believers today unable to possess the same power? *Is there any less demonic activity in today's day and age?*

Jesus appointed the seventy to go out and do exactly what He had been doing—preach the Gospel, heal the sick, and cast out evil spirits (see Luke 10:1).

> *And the seventy returned again with joy, saying, Lord, even the devils are subject unto us through Thy name. And He said unto them, I beheld satan as lightning fall from heaven. Behold, I give unto you power to tread on serpents and scorpions [evil spirits], and over all the power of the enemy: and nothing shall by any means hurt you. Notwithstanding in this rejoice not, that the spirits are subject unto you; but rather rejoice, because your names are written in heaven (Luke 10:17-20).*

Now, at this point, we usually stop reading—*"because your names are written in heaven."* This has been interpreted to mean, *it's not so important for you to cast out devils*; it is more important that your names are written in Heaven. And this is true, but it does not lessen the importance of casting out devils. Read on...

> *In that hour **Jesus rejoiced in spirit**, and said, I thank Thee, O Father, Lord of heaven and earth, that Thou hast hid these things from the wise and prudent, and hast revealed them unto babes: even so, Father; for so it seemed good in Thy sight (Luke 10:21).*

When this Scripture is read in context, you can see what really happened. The seventy went out, and for the first time ever, in any force, the disciples attacked the kingdom of satan. It caused satan to come down from the heavenlies (his realm) so fast that Jesus said he fell "as lightning"!

Then Jesus warned the apostles not to get too confident with themselves; by remembering that they were citizens of Heaven, they were to remember from whom the *power* came that made the demons obey them. Christ still intended for the disciples to continue to cast out devils. But nonetheless, *"in that hour Jesus rejoiced in spirit."* I haven't found any other place in Scripture that tells me that Jesus had as much fun as He did that day! Satan had to contend with only Jesus before; now seventy others were invading his kingdom!

Believers are members of the Body of Christ with a destiny in Heaven. They belong to a supernatural God, and are His children, in fact; therefore, they must also be a supernatural people who should be performing supernatural deeds, including the casting out of devils!

Every believer should be able to cause havoc in satan's realm. When God shows you an enemy, He is introducing you to your future. After all, where would David be without Goliath? On the other hand, if you run from your enemy, you lose your promotion.

Now, if you are still not convinced that the message of deliverance is to *all* believers, then read Mark 16:17-18:

> *And these signs shall follow them that believe; In My name **shall they cast out devils**; they shall speak with new tongues; they shall take up serpents; and if they drink any deadly thing, it shall not hurt them; they shall lay hands on the sick, and they shall recover.*

These were the *last words* of Jesus spoken to the disciples before He ascended into Heaven, and thus, they were *so very important to Him*. Surprisingly, He did not seem to need the use of the admonition, *"Don't look under every bush for the devil."* So, I wonder who planted this expression in the Church? Here's a new declaration for you…*when in doubt, cast it out!*

In Luke 10:17-18, it was "satan"[3] that *"fell as lightning from heaven"* and not *"lucifer"*[4]—two totally different Greek words; therefore, it is not referring to the occasion of lucifer's rebellion and God throwing him out of Heaven, as stated in Isaiah 14:12.

The verse, "I beheld satan as lightning fall from heaven" has in the past been associated with God throwing lucifer out of Heaven. But "lucifer" in the Hebrew dictionary is *hêylêl*, whereas "satan" (the name lucifer received when he was thrown out of Heaven) is spelled *sâtân*. It is *sâtân* that is used in Luke 10:18, meaning that when Jesus saw "satan as lightning fall from heaven," he had *already had his new name*. So, this Scripture could not be referring to lucifer being originally thrown out of Heaven.

The seventy disciples' ability to wreak havoc on satan's kingdom (he'd already set up his kingdom after his fall) caused him to fall as lightning from Heaven to investigate!

Don't you just love that verse?

Again, I stand on the theory that it is very hard to fight your enemy if you do not know his strength, his nature, or his strategy. So, how do we find out how demons operate? In His Word. As we consult the Bible and compile a list of facts about evil spirits/demons, we will discover how satan operates and how he operates the evil spirits, and then we'll know what mankind is up against...before we get rid of them!

EVIL SPIRITS/DEMONS:

▸ Can teach (see 1 Tim. 4:1).

▸ Can tell fortunes (see Acts 16:16).

▸ Can speak (see Mark 1:34; 5:9,12).

▸ Can go in and out of a host body, unless rejected and resisted (see Matt. 12:43-45).

▸ [Thousands of them] can torment a host body at the same time (see Mark 5:9; Luke 8:30).

▸ Can put up a strong fight. However, we are given armor to enable us to fight against them (see Eph. 6:11-12).

Evil spirits, called *familiar spirits* can be passed on in families, from generation to generation (see Lev. 26:39; Isa. 14:21; Jer. 32:18). Have you ever noticed a family where the grandfather is a drunkard, the father is a drunkard, and the son also leans towards drunkenness? Evil spirits like to stay in families, passing down through the generations! Illness and tragedy are also passed on in families in the same way. These are curses you must break when you become a believer, because you never know what might have happened in the lives of your ancestors.

Demons cause:

- Bondage (see Rom. 8:15).

- Deception (see 1 John 4:1-3).

- Error (see 1 Tim. 4:1).

- Lusts (see John 8:44; Eph. 2:2-3).

- Suicide (see Matt. 17:15; John 10:10).

- Jealousy (see 1 Sam. 18:8-10).

- Grievous vexation (see Matt. 15:22; Luke 11:26).

- Enchantments and witchcraft (see 2 Chron. 33:6).

- Sickness (see Matt. 4:24; Acts 10:38; 19:12).

- Torments (see Matt. 4:24; 15:22).

- Convulsions (see Mark 9:20; Luke 9:37-42).

- Insanity (see Matt. 4:24; 17:15).

- Blindness (see Matt. 12:22).

- Dumbness (see Matt. 12:22; 9:32-33).

- Dumbness and deafness (see Mark 9:25).

- False doctrine and worship (see 1 Tim: 4:1; Lev. 17:7; Ps. 106:37).

- Fear (see 2 Tim. 1:7).

- Love of the world (see 1 John 2:16).

- Lust of the eyes (see 1 John 2:16).

- Pride of life (see 1 John 2:16).

- Contention (see 1 Kings 22:21-24).

- False prophesy (see 1 Kings 22:21-24).

- Lying (see 1 Kings 22:21-24).

- They fear God (see James 2:19).

- ◆ They are subject to Jesus Christ (see Matt. 8:16-17; Mark 16:17; Luke 10:17; Acts 19:12).

- ◆ They recognize those who have power over them (see Acts 19:13-17).

- ◆ They have characteristics that make up a knowing being. They walk, hear, seek, see, think, know, oppress, and dwell in a host body to accomplish their evil assignments (see Matt. 12:43-45; Mark 1:23-24; 3:11).

- ◆ Their purpose is to torment believers and mankind in general (see 1 Pet. 5: 8; Rev. 2:10).

Evil spirits/demons, the agents of satan, corrupt the bodies and minds of men and are responsible for every evil, unholy condition and doctrinal error that is known among mankind. These demons do not work willy-nilly; they have a purpose and an aim. The obvious one is to try and completely cripple and destroy mankind and prevent him from accepting the redeeming work of Cavalry; and sometimes their subtleties are not so obvious.

Contact with demons is forbidden in the Word of God:

And the soul that turneth after such as have familiar spirits, and after wizards, to go a-whoring after them, I will even set My face against that soul, and will cut him off from among his people (Leviticus 20:6; see also 19:31).

Let no one be found among you who sacrifices his son or daughter in the fire, who practices divination or sorcery, interprets omens, engages in witchcraft, or casts spells, or who is a medium or spiritist or who consults the dead. Anyone who does these things is detestable to the Lord... (Deuteronomy 18:10-12a NIV; see also Isaiah 8:19; 1 Chronicles 10:13; Acts 16:16; 1 Timothy 4:1; 1 John 4:1-6).

There is a distinct difference with regard to consorting with evil spirits versus the believer gaining knowledge of them with a view to fulfilling the command of Jesus Christ to "cast them out"!

CAN PEOPLE BE DELIVERED FROM EVIL SPIRITS?

Absolutely! Every blood-washed saint is able to obey the Word of God and make demons respond. Several good Christian books have been written on the subject of demons and evil spirits. While some authors account experiences and others categorize the demons, I take a middle line, because although evil spirits like to work in repetitive systems and groups, there is a danger that comes when you try to act on someone else's experience...you leave out the Holy Spirit's guidance.

Certain demons work with several *"strongman"* (main) spirits, and trying to limit them to one specific strongman can lead to many hours of unnecessary ministry to a person seeking deliverance. Each person is a unique individual, and those spirits that are able to torment one person might not be tolerated by another, even though the same type of strongman ultimately operates in their lives.

The first thing that we have to acknowledge is that *all discernment during deliverance should be totally and utterly dependent upon the prompting of the Holy Spirit.*

Sometimes we are unable to understand fully the knowledge that the Holy Spirit gives us, but if we are obedient, we can see a wonderful release in the person being ministered to. The thing that the Holy Spirit moves us to do has far more significance than our human minds can credit. For instance, during one deliverance, when a *spirit of fear* had manifested itself, I was prompted to place my hand on the back of the person being ministered to. Have you ever been scared or fearful? Which part of you feels most vulnerable...your back! If a person doing the ministering is fully under the sway of the Holy Spirit, nothing, I repeat, nothing that you are prompted to do is without significance.

Before a Christian can be used in the area of *discerning of spirits* and the deliverance ministry, they must make sure that their own lives are clean before the Lord. This is a priority. They must wait upon the Spirit of God to show them if their lives are out of order in any way. This is essential; as one can leave no ground for sin in which satan can maneuver.

I have been present when an evil spirit in the one being ministered to, pointed out an exact area in which the one ministering to them was out of order. It immediately undermined the credibility and confidence of the one doing the ministry.

THE STRONGMAN

Initially, let the one in need of deliverance talk for a while, as you wait upon the Holy Spirit to point out the strongman in their lives. It is amazing how evil spirits make themselves known in a man's actions and speech.

The scribes had come down from Jerusalem and accused Jesus of casting out devils by the prince of devils—*Beelzebub.*

> *And He called them unto Him, and said unto them in parables, How can satan cast out satan? And if a kingdom be divided against itself, that kingdom cannot stand....***No man can enter into a strong man's house, and spoil his goods, except he will first bind the strong man; and then he will spoil his house** (Mark 3:23-24,27).

> *But if I cast out devils by the Spirit of God, then the kingdom of God is come unto you. Or else how can one enter into a* **strong man's house, and spoil his goods, except he first bind the strong man?** *and then he will spoil his house* (Matthew 12:28-29).

The strongman must be recognized and overcome before you can easily cast out the lesser devils. I always think of the strongman as being the doorman who keeps the door of man's spirit closed, preventing us from getting to the lesser devils occupying a man's spirit. When we overcome and truss up the doorman (strongman), it leaves the door wide open in order to enter and remove the lesser devils.

> *When a strong man* **armed** *keepeth his palace, his goods are in peace: but when* **a stronger** *than he shall come upon him* [using the name and authority of Jesus Christ], *and overcome him, he taketh from him all his* **armor wherein he trusted**, *and divideth his spoils* (Luke 11:21-22).

With what is a strongman armed (or protected)?

GOD'S ARMOR VERSUS SATAN'S ARMOR

God's Armor	Satan's Armor
Helmet of salvation	Damnation on his head
Breastplate of righteousness	Breastplate of unrighteousness
Loincloth of truth	Loincloth of lies
Shoes of peace	Strife and unbelief
Word of God as a sword	False doctrines and cults
Shield of faith	Spirit of fear

Satan, the embodiment of evil, is the *"strongman's"* source. We understand that the strongman's armor or protection is evil spirits. He surrounds himself with demons that operate in different areas of sin. They accompany and aid the strongman by oppressing or possessing a body—that is, if the owner of the body gives them permission by his behavior. As believers depend on spiritual armor (see Eph. 6) as a protection against evil, so the strongman uses different sets of evil spirits as armor and protection to maintain his home in his host body.

Most strongmen mentioned in the Bible readily identified themselves, and there are also quite a few strongmen not mentioned directly in the Bible. In any case, a list of the main strongmen follows in Chapter 10. As can be noticed from this list, some devils do operate together under *different* strongmen, so it is a futile effort to adamantly categorize them. The Holy Spirit is the one who will ultimately and accurately guide you.

DELIVERANCE

It is not difficult to find who the strongmen are in the Bible, and the manifestations that they produce. But anyone with the gift of discernment will know that quite a few strongmen exist not directly named in the Word of God, like *rejection* and *rebellion*, which are very powerful spirits. Knowledge like this comes through a complete surrendering of *one's own will* and leaving oneself totally dependent upon the power and guidance of the Holy Spirit. His guidance leads to the discerning of the each strongman and complete deliverance. Over a period of time, how the Holy Spirit meets a given situation is repeated over and over again, and a pattern develops.

As stated before, the first prerequisite is to have one's own life *clean* before God. It is also essential that the one who is ministering understands all he is doing, and if a certain situation develops, or something unusual manifests, he should have full confidence in *God*, and be able to stand *firm* and allow the Holy Spirit to move in the situation. It is no good starting to minister and then losing your nerve!

It can be a little unnerving to see a deliverance for the first time; but if a person is deeply rooted in Christ, understands by whose *power* he is working, and always remembers that the Lord has *everything under control*, then it should not be difficult to stand your ground.

If the Holy Spirit prompts you in the gift of discernment, my advice would be not to attempt to minister by yourself, but sit in as a spectator with someone who is experienced. When your confidence builds, ask that person to let you work with him for a while, until you gain assurance during delivery ministry.

This does not mean ultimately working alone; in fact, it is always better to work with another believer. Jesus always sent the disciples out by two's. If you try to do everything yourself, without prior knowledge, you are likely to leave the one being ministered to in a worse state than before you started! All you will have achieved, to say the least, is to stir up a hornet's nest!

Evil spirits are full of deceit and tricks, and will not hesitate to use these qualities if they think you will leave them alone. But remember, that when *a child of God commands an evil spirit to leave a host body, using the name and authority of Jesus Christ*, that demon will be unable to stay there. It *must obey* the believer, as long as the host body *desires and demands that it leave*.

I remember once helping with a ministry deliverance. It was my first time to assist, when a certain spirit had been told to leave its host's body. The person being delivered started to yawn, as she had when other spirits had left. I started "hallelujahing," pleased that the spirit had left. But my coworker never moved a muscle. She just said, "You are not fooling me. I know you are still there, and until I have the witness in my spirit that you have gone, I'll not let up on you." I had been fooled. I had been operating by my eyes, whereas my more experienced partner had been operating by her spirit. Needless to say in a very short time, the spirit "whooped" out!

It is important to know that evil spirits come out of a person in the same way they go in—through the orifices of the body. During deliverance, most come out quietly rather than noisily. That is why you have to be in complete tune with the Holy Spirit to know when they manifest and when they leave.

Sometimes the evil spirits want to "talk," and I have heard of people who carry on a conversation with them, even ask their names; but frankly, I have never felt the desire to speak to them, nor ask questions, as they would probably lie to me anyway. They certainly do not want to willingly cooperate with me to cast them out. If an evil spirit tries to speak through its host's mouth, just tell it to be quiet. It has nothing of interest to say that you want to hear.

Another trick of the devils is to throw the person who is being delivered all over the place, or make them shake uncontrollably; or even as happened once in my presence, the person being delivered started to spin like a top. It is all so unnecessary and is just a ploy to distract you. Simply tell the demon to *be still in Jesus' name.*

Often, the devils cause the one being delivered to throw up; or else they put up such a battle when being cast out that they internally tear the one being delivered, and pain is felt. Again, as Christ's ambassador, you have the authority to tell the spirit to *come out quietly without tearing* the person.

When an evil spirit reveals itself, it is quite common for the person being delivered to experience the feeling of that spirit manifesting in them. In other words, if a spirit of anger or rage is being cast out, the one being delivered might suddenly feel very angry and aggressive towards the one who is ministering to them. Don't get shaken if the person starts to verbally abuse you; just determinedly resist the spirit until it leaves. All feelings of anger and animosity will leave with it when it departs.

It is also quite common, when you are ministering to a person, to find someone else in the party being delivered of the same kind of spirit at the same time. However, don't let yourself get sidetracked; stick to what you are doing.

WHERE DO THE EVIL SPIRITS GO WHEN CAST OUT?

As Jesus was casting out the evil spirits in the man of Gadarene in Mark 5:12-13a,

> *...all the devils besought Him, saying, Send us into the swine, that we may enter into them. And forthwith Jesus gave them leave. And the unclean spirits went out, and entered into the swine.*

Jesus allowed the unclean spirits to go into the pigs—not because He didn't like pigs, but to give us another vital piece of information. The demons looked for another home immediately!

> *When the unclean spirit is gone out of a man, he walketh through dry places, seeking rest; and finding none, he saith, I will return unto my house* [host body] *whence I came out* (Luke 11:24).

These disembodied spirits are of no use unless working through a human or animal. Hence, when you are ministering deliverance, it is better to work in two's; while one is ministering, the other is sending the unclean spirits that leave the host body to waterless (dry) places. That's the way to do it. Send them back to waterless or dry places. If there are any unsaved people or animals in close vicinity, the evil spirits being cast out will find it very convenient to attach themselves to them. Therefore, we need to protect them by sending the evil spirits to dry places.

Do not try to cast out a devil from a person unless you first have that person's consent and knowledge. The spirit has every legal right to stay where it is if its host body is willing to give it a home. Never cast out a demon from an unsaved person, for if they do not fill themselves with the Word of God after deliverance, a more devastating outcome will result, as we notice in the following Scripture:

> *I will return unto my house whence I came out. And when he cometh, he findeth it swept and garnished. Then goeth he, and taketh to him seven other spirits more wicked than himself; and they enter in, and dwell there: and the last state of that man is worse than the first* (Luke 11:24b-26).

So, what do you do if someone manifests a demon/evil spirit but is not saved? You can "bind" that demon, rendering it harmless and ineffective, in Jesus' name. In other words, you have made the demon ineffective, but it still resides within the person. The demon/evil spirit is not being cast out of the host body; otherwise, he might find the host body cleansed of all evil, and because the Word of God has not filled the space made vacant by his removal, he could take back seven devils worse than himself, as the Scripture in Luke warns! By binding him, however, you merely make the evil spirit ineffective, or put it in "cold storage" until a later date when the host body decides to be set free after accepting the Lord as his Savior and when proper ministry can take place. Binding has to be done on a daily basis as the Lord reminds us, "Give us this day our daily bread" (Matt. 6:11); whereas casting out a devil from a saved person is done only once, unless the believer lets it in again.

Please do not use the foregoing information to act independently. If you do not know for sure that you are called to the "discerning of spirits" ministry, then get some help from those who have been given the ministry.

ENDNOTES

1. *Parallel New Testament in Greek and English*, by Zondervan, pg 751.

2. *Parallel New Testament in Greek and English*, by Zondervan, pg 161.

3. *Strong's Concordance*, 7854.

4. *Strong's Concordance*, 1966.

9

HOW DOES THE DEVIL KNOW EXACTLY WHAT TEMPTATION WILL WORK ON YOU?

For 30 years I dug in the Word with this question before I found the answer. My question was: *How is it that the devil knows exactly in which area each man is most vulnerable, and exactly how to tempt him most effectively in that area?*

How does satan know our weak points? How does he know just where to hit us where it hurts the most? No two men are alike; what tempts one will not tempt another. One man can be crippled in a certain area, while another can withstand a temptation in the same area. But how does the devil specialize in pinpointing a weakness and knowing exactly which area to hone in on in order to cripple a particular person?

Satan is not like God; he is not omnipresent (all places at the same time) or omniscient (knowing everything, having all knowledge). He is only a *created being*. God created him, and it was satan's own decision to rebel. So, how can he keep tabs on everybody, Christians and non-Christians alike...and know each of their individual weaknesses?

We show him!

How? By our *spiritual clothing*—what we wear! We are temporarily in earthbound bodies, but we do our warfare in the heavenly realms—on satan's turf, as it were. He has the ability to see in that realm, whereas we don't...so we have to operate in faith. This ability gives him an advantage; however, armed with the following knowledge, we can now change so that we even the odds.

SPIRITUAL CLOTHING

Let's look at the parable of the wedding feast in Matthew 22:1-10. The wedding guests who were originally invited made excuses and refused to attend the wedding. Consequently, the king sent his servants into the highways to gather "good and bad" guests (see verse 10). The guests who were found on the highways in this parable did not have the appropriate wedding clothing prepared in advance, so the King *offered them* all the required wedding clothing. Notice verse 11:

> *And when the king came in to see the guests, he saw there a man which had not on a wedding garment* [one man obviously insulted the king by neglecting to wear the garment provided]: *and he saith unto him, Friend, how comest thou in hither not having a wedding garment? And he was speechless* (Matthew 22:11-12).

The king wanted to know how the man had gotten into the celebrations without wearing the necessary garment, but the man had no excuse.

> *Then said the king to the servants, Bind him hand and foot, and take him away, and cast him into outer darkness; there shall be weeping and gnashing of teeth* (Matthew 22:13).

The guest was bound and sent to outer darkness! This seems a little extreme, unless you look at it in the spiritual context. God does not have any favorites; neither did this king. The earthly king offered wedding attire; Jesus clothes us in salvation and righteousness—our wedding attire. It was the man himself and his *choice of clothes* that decided his destiny! And so it is with mankind—man makes his choices and is clothed accordingly.

There is a lesson to be learned here about clothing and its importance and significance in the heavenlies. Let's look at some Scriptures.

> *And he showed me Joshua the high priest standing before the angel of the Lord, and satan standing at his right hand to resist him. And the Lord said unto satan, The Lord rebuke thee, O satan....Now Joshua was clothed with filthy garments, and stood before the angel. And he answered and spake unto those that stood before him, saying, Take away the filthy garments from him [Joshua]. And unto him he said, Behold, I have caused thine iniquity to pass from thee, and I will clothe thee with change of raiment* (Zechariah 3:1-4).

Joshua was a soldier and high priest, constantly in God's presence. Daily he dialogued with Him, so there is no way he would have appeared before the Lord with earthly "dirty priest clothing," yet God *had to* clean him up. *God was not looking at Joshua's earthly clothes, but at his spiritual ones*...and so was satan. He felt confident enough to resist Joshua because of what he was wearing!

Let's take a closer look at spiritual (heavenly) clothing—the kind we cannot see with our human eyes, but every being in the spiritual realm can see!

> *I counsel thee to buy of me gold tried in the fire, that thou mayest be rich;* **and white raiment, that thou mayest be clothed, and that the shame of thy nakedness do not appear**... (Revelation 3:18).

God Is Clothed

God also has spiritual clothing in the heavenly realms.

> *Bless the Lord, O my soul. O Lord my God, Thou art very great; Thou art clothed with honor and majesty. Who coverest Thyself with light as with a garment* (Psalm 104:1-2a).

> *The Lord reigneth, He is* **clothed with** *majesty; the Lord is* **clothed with** *strength, wherewith He hath girded Himself*... (Psalm 93:1).

Jesus Is Clothed

*For He put on **righteousness as a** breastplate, and an **helmet of** salvation upon his head; and he put on the **garments of vengeance for clothing, and was clad with zeal as a cloak*** (Isaiah 59:17).

Angels Are Clothed

...suddenly two men in clothes that gleamed like lightning stood be-side them [the two men standing guard at the tomb of Jesus had on shining garments—their holiness] (Luke 24:4 NIV).

Believers Are Clothed

*For He hath **clothed me** with the **garments of salvation**, He hath **covered me** with the **robe of righteousness**...* (Isaiah 61:10b).

*Let Thy priests, O Lord God, be **clothed with salvation**...* (2 Chronicles 6:41b).

*I will also **clothe** her priests with **salvation*** (Psalm 132:16a).

*Let thy priests be **clothed** with **righteousness*** (Psalm 132:9a).

*I put on **righteousness**, and it **clothed me**: my **judgment** was as a **robe and a diadem*** (Job 29:14).

Garments of Praise

*My son, hear the instruction of thy father, and forsake not the law of thy mother: for they shall be an **ornament of grace** unto thy **head, and chains about thy neck*** [spiritual jewelry] (Proverbs 1:8-9).

Speaking about wisdom:

*She shall give to thine **head an ornament of grace: a crown of glory** shall she deliver to thee* (Proverbs 4:9).

Speaking of a good wife:

***Strength** and **honor** are her clothing* (Proverbs 31:25a).

*...Yea, all of you be subject one to another, and be **clothed with humility**...* (1 Peter 5:5).

*Whose adorning let it not be that outward adorning of plaiting the hair, and of wearing of gold, or of putting on of apparel; but let it be the hidden man of the heart, in that which is not corruptible, even the **ornament of a meek and quiet spirit**, which is in the sight of God of great price* (1 Peter 3:3-4).

*And to her was granted that she should be **arrayed** in fine linen, clean and white: for the fine linen is the **righteousness** of saints* (Revelation 19:8).

Garments of Sin

*The king shall mourn, and the prince shall be **clothed with desolation**...* (Ezekiel 7:27).

*Let them be **clothed with shame and dishonor** that magnify themselves against me* (Psalm 35:26b).

*Therefore **pride** compasseth them about **as a chain; violence** covereth them as a **garment*** (Psalm 73:6).

*As he **clothed** himself with **cursing** like as with his **garment**...* (Psalm 109:18).

*Let mine adversaries be **clothed** with **shame**, and let them cover themselves with their own **confusion**, as with a **mantle*** (Psalm 109:29).

*They that hate thee shall be **clothed** with **shame**...* (Job 8:22).

*Then all the princes of the sea shall come down from their thrones, and lay away their robes, and put off their broidered garments: they shall **clothe** themselves with **trembling**...* (Ezekiel 26:16).

*For neither at any time used we flattering words, as ye know, nor a **cloak** of **covetousness**...* (1 Thessalonians 2:5).

What we clothe ourselves with is clearly seen in the heavenlies. If we are depressed and heavy, we wear the appropriate robes. Accordingly, satan sees it and knows it is a good time to attack.

God advised, *"Put on a **garment of praise** for a **spirit of heaviness!"*** (Isa. 61:3b, author's paraphrase). Praise is often the last thing you want to do when you are depressed, but God knows that satan can see you clothed in heaviness in the heavenly realm. Therefore, God advises you to start praising so that satan doesn't attack you when you are feeling low. Even the weakest of praise will put a different set of clothes on you! Keep your garments fresh; don't walk around with moth-eaten robes in the heavenlies.

> Behold, I come as a thief. Blessed is he that watcheth, and **keepeth his garments**, lest he walk naked, and they see his shame (Revelation 16:15).

Garments of War

Without a garment of righteousness you cannot wear your armor.

> Wherefore take unto you the whole armor of God, that ye may be able to withstand in the evil day, and having done all, to stand. Stand therefore, having your **loins girt about with truth**, and having on the **breastplate of righteousness**; and your **feet shod** with the preparation of the gospel of peace; above all, taking the **shield of faith**, wherewith ye shall be able to quench all the fiery darts of the wicked. And take the **helmet of salvation**, and the **sword of the Spirit**, which is the word of God (Ephesians 6:13-17).

We have to understand our heavenly clothing depends upon our spiritual health and obedience. This clothing is what is seen by heavenly beings. It is also how satan knows the specific areas in which to attack mankind! When a believer is strong in an area, satan leaves him alone in that area; but if he does not always adhere to God's Word and His ways, his spiritual clothing will expose him and reveal his vulnerability in the respective areas.

Satan will be very quick to zoom in on any weak areas. However, you can level the advantage of the satanic realms' ability to see in the heavenlies, by making a concentrated effort to make sure you are always dressed in the appropriate godly clothing, leaving no area for satan to zone in on.

So, if at any time your Christian walk is faulty and you think no one knows, remember you are *transparent in the heavenlies*!

SATANIC INVASION

There are many ways an evil spirit can enter. Before we enumerate the main spirit manifestations, I would like to expand a little on how they can enter a body and the areas in which they freely operate. Man's need to dabble in the supernatural, if not channeled to Christianity, is destined to cause severe oppression by evil spirits.

Satanism dates as long back in history as does Christianity, with many names perpetuating this ancient cult—names like the French knight, Gilles de Rais. In the 1400's, he shocked the world with his confession before he died—he had used over 800 children in satanic ritualistic sacrifices.

French priest, Urbain Grandier, used the nuns of a local convent in his orgies to celebrate Black Masses. If the nuns became pregnant, these babies were used as satanic sacrifices.

Britain was scandalized when Sir Francis Dashwood's infamous Hell Fire Club was established during the 18th century. He freely admitted evoking the devil in his black mass ceremonies and claimed he appeared in either the form of a black cat or goat-like figure. The Hell Fire Club numbered members of royalty and aristocracy, members of the government (he himself was the Chancellor of the Exchequer), and even included professors, poets, and famous painters.

On *Walpurgisnacht*, which is the traditional witches "Sabbat," the First Church of Satan was established in San Francisco by Anton Szandor LaVey. Things were quiet until 1966 when Anton Szandor LaVey, a former animal trainer in the circus, produced two books, *The Satanic Rituals* and *The Satanic Bible* which proved to be instant best-sellers.

A more dangerous group called "The Temple of Set" founded by Michael Aquino claimed to show the world the advantages and ethics of the "dark arts." Even more evil secret organizations were birthed, such as The Golden Dawn, the O.T.O, and the Illuminati who practiced black magic.

During the 70's and 80's, there were a series of murders committed by young men who claimed that satanism inspired them and *The Satanic Bible* was their motivation.

Satanists have three basic books, *The Satanic Bible*, *The Satanic Rituals*, and *The Book of Shadows*. Many people have not realized that the advisor on the film, *Rosemary's Baby*, was no other than LaVey, in which he had a small part playing the devil himself. Later, he assisted the director of a movie starring John Travolta, called *The Devil's Rain*. LaVey used this association with the film industry to increase the number of followers.

Regrettably, in that year, the sale of the Satanic Bibles equaled that of the Christian Bibles in America! What a sad indictment against mankind.

Aleister Crowley, head of the British Satanists, during the era of the "Jack the Ripper" murders, claimed that a young man named D'Onston, a professed satanist, was responsible for the murders. But nothing was done about it!

Satanist John Kilminster rekindled the English Church of Satan by putting an advertisement in the local paper. Kilminster provided do-it-yourself werewolf kits for his new recruits! He held his first meeting in a nearby Little Chef fast-food restaurant. The coven was comprised mostly of middle-aged men and women with abnormal sexual interests.

This sounds ridiculous, but consider how these people have influenced our world and lives. They have succeeded in securing places of power, and over a period of time, they have managed to remove Christian religion from schools in America and England; yet education boards have eagerly embraced books on witches, black magic, tarot cards, and crystal balls. They have permeated all strata of society, film, television, and books, and have introduced anything that deviates and distracts a child's mind before he or she can be established in the Christian belief. So be diligent and aware for the sake of your families.

HOW DO PEOPLE GET INVOLVED?

Satanism

Usually a person's desire to know more about the supernatural causes the first step towards satanism. He or she will usually start with books on the supernatural, which they read avidly. Talking about the books causes people of like interests to gather around. (Satanists are always on the lookout for new converts.) A satanist will invite them to a meeting, and of their own free will, they will attend.

There is no doubt that they will see a manifestation of the supernatural, and as one's soul craves for this, they are hooked! If they show real interest, they are asked to join the satanic circle, and be initiated. Typically, if they accept, they are taken to a coven, where members will be dressed in white, red, or black robes, or even naked (depending on the coven.) There is an altar on which stands the cult's image of satan, usually a goat-like creature with a human body and horns. The worshippers carry torches that have been lit from the flame between the horns or legs of the idol; and a cup containing hallucinogenic herbs mixed with alcohol is drunk.

At an initiation ritual, the initiate will stand naked before a sacrificial altar. He stands before the "high priest" (who is supposed to represent the devil) and is asked to recite the Lord's prayer backwards. He is given their "holy communion," wherein he takes stolen communion wafers and stomps on them. Next, he takes the chalice of wine, supposedly the blood of Jesus Christ. Sometimes he is asked to urinate into the same cup. There are other things put into the cup, too vile to mention. More often than not a naked woman lies on the altar with a pentagon drawn on her belly. The initiate stands to one side of the altar, and the high priest on the other side. The high priest drinks from the chalice, and then the initiate drinks from it. The initiate is handed an upside-down cross and breaks the arms off it. The priest then puts a necklace around the initiate's neck; it has a pentagram on it which has been "blessed " by the high priest and his followers. They chant over it. Each necklace has its own evil spirit attached to it.

Women are usually attracted to satanism by the power they can receive, whereas men are attracted by the sex and perversion. Anyone who has gone this far into satanism is already in deep water. Demons are called up regularly at satanic meetings, and the vilest orgies take place under the influence of drugs and heavy rock music. Direct contact with the devil can be made!

atanists use the Ouija board, a game where supposedly the spirits the dead communicate with the living. This is satan's attempt to gain the player's attention, but in reality is contact with evil disembodied spirits who give information and predictions to gain one's confidence and trust and draw one in, with the intention of eventually taking possession. Remember that satan gives and does nothing for free and will eventually call in his marker and either possess the initiate or kill him.

Spiritism/Spiritualism

Mankind longs for the supernatural, with many traditional Christians dabbling in spiritualism. The Roman Catholic Church, especially in Brazil, participates in spiritualism during their regular church services (according to the May 1983 issue of World Vision's publication "Intercessors International").

Unlike satanism, spiritualism plays on the concern of a person for a dead loved one, entrapping many with the hope that death is not the final link and that communication with a loved one can continue after death. This "church" comes in as an "angel of light" by using the Bible freely, but misconstrues the Scriptures for its own ends.

A medium or spiritualist acts as a channel between the dead and the one seeking a loved one. These meetings are called séances. Spiritualists start and end their meetings with a prayer leading many into deception by their apparent "good" acts. Those who fall for their deception become even more deeply involved and deluded. They are given a "personal guide," or more correctly, a familiar spirit (demon) that is supposed to befriend, protect, and guide them. Paintings, pictures, and photographs are used, and evil spirits attach themselves to these. These paintings and pictures are taken by the initiate into his own home, and they become his "household gods."

> Then ye shall drive out all the inhabitants of the land from before you, and destroy all their pictures, and destroy all their molten images, and quite pluck down all their high places (Numbers 33:52).

> Thou shalt have no other gods before Me. Thou shalt not make unto thee any graven image, or any likeness of **any thing** that is in heaven above, or that is in the earth beneath, or that is in the water

*under the earth: thou shalt not bow down thyself to them, nor serve them: for I the Lord thy God **am** a jealous God, visiting the iniquity of the fathers upon the children unto the third and fourth **genera-tion** of them that hate Me* (Exodus 20:3-5).

This is one of the most dangerous of "churches." They counterfeit the genuine gifts from God, even to the laying on of hands for heal-ing. You might say, "Ah, but sometimes the illness does leave when these people lay hands on members." Of course, it will—temporarily. It was satan who put the sickness on the member in the first place; so, it is quite simple for him to take it away. It is well worth him doing so, especially if he manages to deceive a person by this counterfeit move and gets a grip on the soul of a possible new member!

Eastern Religions

A personal *guru* always introduces followers to the Eastern religions.

Meditation (called Transcendental Meditation)

During the 1960's and the "flower power era," anything Eastern became trendy. The Beatles group publicized Maharishi. Mahesh Yogi, born Mahesh Srivastava in Jabalpur, became their Maharishi (spiritual guide). He then took it upon himself to spread the tech-niques of transcendental meditation (TM) from spiritual masters in the Himalayas who had made him a Yogi. A European research uni-versity in Switzerland was named after him, where he established research into human consciousness. His British headquarters is Mentmore Tower in Buckinghamshire, which he bought from the Queen for 250 million pounds, which he could well afford after American universities included TM in their courses and he opened and controlled more than 4000 TM centers in 150 countries. Chris-tians—beware! This seemingly harmless meditation is the art of emptying oneself and concentrating on one's inner self, getting in touch with one's inner self to find inner peace. Note the key word here is *"self,"* which is directly opposed to what the Word of God says when God teaches us to think of others and meet the needs of others before self. It is believed that the word *om*, which the initiate chants, is an abbreviation for the "three in one"—the omniscient (all-knowing), omnipotent (all-powerful), and the omnipresent (everywhere present). This is blasphemy; only Almighty God has these attributes. Through emptying one's self, one is wide open to satanic invasion. When you take control of a man's mind, you have all of him.

Yogi/Yoga (meditation, Hinduism, idolatry)

A Hindu philosophy practiced by Brahmins is to keep a strict spiritual control over their own deepest feelings and desires with the aim of gaining occult powers and becoming one with the universal spirit.

Yoga is sold to the world as a way to relax the mind and body. Anyone who says that they are into yoga for the exercise only is deluded. Ignorance of the demonic activity behind this seemingly harmless form of relaxation and exercise will not protect followers of yoga. They will still be in danger of falling under heavy demon possession because all the exercises are given by demons. The mind being "evacuated" of godly thoughts is wide open for demon invasion, same as in meditation.

Hindus

Hindus believe in the caste system, a social organization, and the cycles of reincarnation.

The Hindus practice a ceremony called "poo kulithal," or simply, fire walking! This ceremony takes place in mid-March or mid-April, the month of Panguni on the Hindu calendar. For 18 days prior to the ceremony, followers fast, pray, abstain from cigarettes and alcohol, and are celibate. After a prayer at the temple, the devotees make their way to a river. With more prayer, songs, and ceremonial drums, they are supposedly purified in water in a form of baptism. Crescendos of the chanters sink the devotees into a trance or a complete state of self-hypnosis by mid-morning. This is very necessary for the piercings that follow.

The devotees are pierced with large silver or copper hooks, usually with brass containers or coconuts or other citrus fruits attached. These are hooked into the devotee's back and arms, and also into the cheeks and tongue. Yet these believers, in a state of deep hypnosis, supposedly do not bleed or feel any pain. They are already under the influence of demons that love to corrupt the minds and flesh of mankind and whose ultimate aim is to get the initiates to walk across a bed of burning embers already glowing in a pit that is 15 meters by 4 meters. Anyone who can walk unharmed across burning embers is obviously under the power of a strong being. And remember, God never calls us to do tricks like this. God does not test us, nor are we to test Him with exploits like these.

Most Hindus maintain that this ceremony dates back to ancient times, when the gods and goddesses ruled the continent of India. The elders say that this ceremony came into being when a believer was asked to demonstrate his devotion to the Mother Draupadi by walking across a bed of fire.

> *And thou shalt not let any of thy seed pass through the fire to Molech, neither shalt thou profane the name of thy God: I am the Lord* (Leviticus 18:21).

Hindus also believe in reincarnation.

> *…it is appointed unto men **once** to die, but after this the judgment* (Hebrews 9:27).

This reincarnation religion is a cop-out; in other words, if you make a mess of this life, you can come back again and have another try, until you eventually reach perfection! No man can reach perfection by himself. God has said that only salvation and a man's willingness, guided by the power of the Holy Spirit can put him on the road to being perfect! You only have to look at the present world to see that for all their "reincarnations," of trying in their own strength to become perfect, this world, in the natural, is going from bad to worse!

Cult Churches

We will see more and more bondage cults, such as Jonestown, Moonie Church, and the church at Waco, spring up as time gets nearer to the return of our Lord Jesus. The idea behind these cults is to seize mind control of its devotees and deprive them in all areas until their *will* is broken. Sadly, the devotees do not realize that they are in such bondage, and readily follow the leader…sometimes even to their deaths.

Unfortunately, television, books, and films depict the fanaticism of these, and the world at large chooses to include Christianity when depicting these cults. Apparently, anyone with zeal and fervor for God is a "fanatic," no matter what their religious beliefs are.

Hare Krishna

This religion is the brainchild of Srila Prabhupada, born in 1896 in Calcutta, whose parents were followers of Krishna. Srila dedicated his life to Krishna at the age of six years. He worked for a chemical plant in Calcutta and in his spare time studied under swami Sri Bhaktisddhanta Sarawati, who told him to "translate and print books and carry *Krishna consciousness* to the world."

He arrived in New York in 1965 and within a year had a dozen initiates. Disciples had to renounce all earthly things and follow the spiritual way. It wasn't long before the shaven-headed, orange-robed followers were a regular sight on the streets of America. He then concentrated on England and set up his headquarters in Hertfordshire after buying George Harrison's country house. By the time he died, he had established over 200 Krishna consciousness centers around the world.

This cult uses meditation that leads to demon possession. *Hare* means "praise," whereas *Krishna* in Hinduism means the last incarnation of Vishnu[1] or, in the Hindi language, means trinity, the preserver of life, which supposedly permeates and sustains the universe. Once again, mind and body bondage delude the devotee into trying to be one with all things in the universe.

> *I am Alpha and Omega, the beginning and the ending, saith the Lord, which is, and which was, and which is to come, the Almighty* (Revelation 1:8; see also Revelation 21:6; 22:13).

Stages of the Cobra

Some covens have their own chants, but for the most part, the universal chant is "om." They take their readings from the Bagvatvita. Devotees go into a self-hypnotic trance and are supposed to project their spirit through space, and at each stage it meets up with some obstacle. If in their spirit they can overcome the obstacle, they can rest and try later for the next stage, which will be a little more difficult than the previous stage. If at any time they fail to overcome the obstacle, their spirit can supposedly be molested in space and the person is left with mental illness or paranoid behavior, with illusions.

Actually what happens is the person leaves himself wide open to demonic oppression and possession, and the *spirit of fear* enters in, causing mental illness.

The ultimate or last *stage of the cobra* always has a *cobra* as its obstacle. Devotees slip into a hypnotic state and prepare to release their spirits into space, this time to face the cobra, the ultimate test. The cobra will allegedly stare hypnotically into the devotee's eyes for hours, and the devotee mentally has to defend himself; but unfortunately, he is handicapped because he is emptied of any movement caused by self-hypnotism. The serpent, being satan's representative, sits ready to strike and spit out its venom. The result is death. If the devotee does happen to survive the venom spat out by the cobra, it still permeates his spirit, and his spirit takes on the cobra's character of evil. Of course, in reality, hypnotism has simply opened up this deluded person to satanic invasion.

Astral Travel

Astral travel allegedly has to do with a spirit leaving a man's body at will and theoretically traveling to a higher state of being. It can also float around in space. But according to the Word of God, only at death does the spirit leave the body; so, it is a *deceptive spirit* that is imitating this astral travel.

Devotees believe a silver cord is attached between the body and the spirit. They believe that when one is astral traveling and someone calls him back into his body too quickly, this cord can be broken, and death can occur. Also, this religion claims that sometimes the silver cords of the devotees can get entangled with another traveler when both are astral traveling out of their bodies at the same time. The result can be one's spirit finishing up in someone else's body! They give the example of Joan of Arc. They say that her silver cord got entangled with a man's; that is why she wanted to fight wars instead of cook and clean in her kitchen! Mind you, she did burn as a witch, so there must be a moral in there somewhere! In astral travel, this swapping of cords is a lie. This sect and belief leads to total demon possession.

Hypnosis

The Bible refers to a man who practices hypnosis as a "charmer," Hypnosis is the art of making a subject extremely susceptible to another's will and involves an induced type of sleep where the devotee's will is under the control of another. The taking away of man's free will can lead to demonic possession.

Hypnosis is supposed to be a science, but *no man should take control over another man's mind*. This practice has been deemed acceptable and is even being promoted in the medical world today as a way to relieve medical conditions. However, *no Christian should ever allow himself to be hypnotized, even upon medical advice*.

There is a never-ending list of cults, and those given here are not in-depth studies; but note, *no man can find God through himself*.

African Witchcraft

There has been very little written about the witchcraft in Africa. It is very involved, but we will cover it lightly.

Voodooism

Voodoo is a mixture of several religions brought to the Caribbean by slaves from Africa. It is made up mostly of ancestral worship and animism; this mixture was then brought back, and initiates settled in the Congo. These slaves, called "Maroons," rebelled in 1758, and the Maroon leaders wrote the "Voodoo Declaration of Independence" in which the slaves were encouraged to slay their masters.

This is the most evil of all cults. It is a heritage from the Canaanites and giant races, and is widely spread all over Africa. Spells are cast and effigies used to destroy recipients. Evil spirits are in total control of this cult.

Devotees believe in ritual healings and exorcisms. If anyone has a problem or sickness, an animal is sacrificed. They usually use a black cockerel, and its blood must be applied to the sickness while the animal is still alive. That way they believe that the evil spirit is drawn out; and then the cockerel is flung into the fire, and that supposedly kills the spirit.

Zombies are usually the result of the voodoo priest alchemist, who injects a man with a nerve-paralyzing toxin, which plunges the victim into a catatonic state. These zombies are greatly feared and are usually the obedient slaves of the priest. People fear the power of the priests, superstitiously believing that the priest has stolen the zombie's soul!

Sangoma/IGqirha (Witchdoctor)

Evil spirits motivate all witchdoctors. *Makosi* are their ancestors (forefathers) and play an important role in the life of the tribes. The Sangoma/IGqirha act as intermediaries between the people and Uthixo, their god, to whom they bring all their ailments or problems.

Ancestral worship is big in Africa and holds many people in bondage. Their ancestors must constantly be appeased, and the poorest of devotees are expected to part with great sums of money for animal sacrifices to their ancestors. This cult is evil and would-be devotees/clients who consult the IGqirha are wide open to demonic oppression.

The IGqirha takes a vile concocted medicine, called *ukupehla*, to help him remember his dreams (theoretically a direct link with the devotee's ancestors) as these play a large part of any diagnosis of the witchdoctors. The client is urged to stay close to the words and customs of the Makosi (their ancestors), as it is important to stay in touch with the source of this spiritual energy.

The Sangoma/IGqirha thinks he is being used as a holistic healer and a protector spirit to the African tribes. Clients come to him if they think there is a curse against them or if they believe the reason for their sickness is because someone has laid a spell on them. If they are unable to have children, or are unlucky in love, or even if an infestation of ticks or lice is in their homes, they take their problems to the Sangoma/IGqirha.

Some Sangomas use snuff, causing them to sneeze, as an aid to diagnosis—they interpret the sneeze fluid. They tell fortunes, make predictions, and foretell future events. If necessary, the Sangoma makes medication to lift the curse from his client. He consults his client's ancestors who are supposed to protect members of their own family, then he makes "muthi" (medicine) from herbs, the bark of trees, and the fat, meat, and blood of animals. He supposedly uses the recipe from his ancestors, which he uses as an antidote against the alleged curse made against his client.

The Sangoma learns most of his "arts" directly from voodooism.

He "divines" who has put a sickness on his client, and usually asks if the client wants him to send the sickness or curse back to the one who sent it. He has the power to do that. The Sangoma also puts needles and nails into an effigy in the same manner as is done in voodooism—to extract revenge. In the process of time, the recipient is supposed to fall ill exactly as described by the Sangoma.

He can also *cast a curse* by using hair or nail parings from the one who originally caused the curse or simply send the primary curse back to the one who originally sent it!

These Sangomas and ancestral worship are so deeply embedded in the African culture that if the Sangoma tells his client that his ancestors are telling him to go and kill a person who is laying a supposed curse on them, they will do it. They do not consider it murder, but merely a ritualistic killing.

The Sangoma makes no pretense of doing good and is a very feared and powerful man in the tribe. Obviously, he is the last person you would want to get on the wrong side of, as he is in the undisputed position to get rid of any enemies!

Ritual dancing and chanting to a hypnotic frenzy by the witchdoctors and their followers open them up to demon possession. Most black people fear the power of the Sangoma/IGqirha. His profession is supposed to be "good" or "white" magic, but is obviously controlled by evil.

Remember, no spiritual activity outside of the Lord God Almighty is good, even though it appears so.

In the New South Africa, this diabolical Sangoma/IGqirha has been accepted as an alternative medical practitioner! Please pray for South Africa.

Inyanga

Inyanga uses divination by bones called *amatambo*. He works on the same principles and rituals as the Sangoma, but uses the "throwing of the bag of bones" to get his diagnosis and guidance.

Abatakathi

Abatakathi is an evil satanic wizard. Just as the Sangoma is used theoretically for "good" spirits, or medicine, so the Abatakathi is his evil counterpart. They can supposedly transfer the spirit from a dead body into a living one, as an appeasement to their ancestors, believing that they can resurrect the spirit of an ancestor who can continue to live in a new body.

These evil ancestral spirits are called *tokolosh*, and are greatly feared among the ancestral worship followers, who are a very superstitious people. The Abatakathi are reverently feared amongst their devotees. They make no pretense of being good and put curses on and seek the death of any who get in their way.

Most black people who believe in this culture use animal skins for amulets, bracelets, or headbands as a talisman to ward off evil.

ENDNOTE

1. *Collins English Dictionary.*

10

STRONGMEN AND THEIR MANIFESTATIONS

SPIRIT OF WITCHCRAFT

Then said Saul unto his servants, Seek me a woman that hath a familiar spirit, that I may go to her, and inquire of her. And his servants said to him, Behold, there is a woman that hath a familiar spirit at Endor (1 Samuel 28:7).

All satanic spirits are evil, but this one is the worst of all. If you ask a believer if he has ever had any contact with this foul spirit, the answer would be an incredulous "No!" Yet many people have unknowingly, in one way or another, dabbled in this the most vicious of spirits, the *spirit of witchcraft.*

Anyone who has dabbled in the satanic realm or has been involved in any of the previous pages of groupings of evil would be a likely candidate for this spirit of witchcraft.

Witchcraft falls under and can be recognized in three basic categories.

▸ Domination.

▸ Manipulation.

▸ Condemnation.

A spirit of witchcraft motivates anyone who operates in any of the above. *Any authority without compassion is oppression* and falls under this spirit.

Manifestations

Manifestations include *participating in any illegal activity within the evil spiritual realm.*

- **Pride**: People in witchcraft often become a law unto themselves.

- **Power**: To rule by fear.

- **Violence**: Takes on the character of his father, the devil.

- **Control**: Dominates and intimidates others.

- **Domination**: Wants absolute control.

- **Delusion**: Unsound doctrine and morals.

- **Deception**: Deceives others and themselves into believing they are always right. This can lead to the person being manipulated, dominated, or condemned, falling under a spirit of bondage, as this spirit of witchcraft works tirelessly to break one down both bodily and spiritually, and works hand-in-glove with a spirit of bondage.

- **Condemnation**.

- **Manipulation**.

- **Wizard**: One entirely under the control of satan.

- **Witch**: Female counterpart of the above.

- **Witchdoctor**: One under the control of satan.

- **Satanist**: God's arch enemy.

- **Self**: Is the primary concern of the one who practices witchcraft.

THE SPIRIT OF DIVINATION/FAMILIAR SPIRIT

And he caused his children to pass through the fire in the valley of the son of Hinnom: also he observed times, and used enchantments, and used witchcraft, and dealt with a familiar spirit, and with wizards: he wrought much evil in the sight of the Lord, to provoke him to anger (2 Chronicles 33:6).

There shall not be found among you any one that maketh his son or his daughter to pass through the fire, or that useth divination, or an observer of times [horoscopes], *or an enchanter, or a witch, or a charmer* [hypnotist], *or a consulter with familiar spirits* [spiritist], *or a wizard, or a necromancer* [consulting with the dead] (Deuteronomy 18:10-11).

Manifestations

◆ **Witch** or **wizard** (a diviner): One who practices the art of sorcery.

◆ **Medium** or **Abatakathi** (African culture): One used to call up evil spirits, usually by the use of a familiar spirit.

◆ **Enchanter/Sangoma/Igquirhi** (African culture): One who makes spells or curses.

◆ **Fortune-telling**: One who uses stars, crystal balls, tea leaves, or the palm to supposedly foretell the future. (Only God has the ability to foretell the future.)

◆ **Divination of entrails** (see Ezek. 21:21).

◆ **Divination by arrows** (see Ezek. 21:21).

◆ **Divination by rod** or **stick** (see Hos. 4:12).

◆ **Divination by bones**: Amatambo or Inyanga (African culture).

◆ **Divination by snuff** (African culture).

◆ **Clairvoyant**: One who supposedly reads the future, using cards, tea leaves, your palm, or a crystal ball, etc.

- **Hypnotist**: One who controls the mind of another by putting him in a hypnotic trance.

- **Demonolatry**: The worship of evil spirits (African culture), i.e. "tokolosh."

- **Ancestral worship** (African culture): Calling up the ancestral spirits.

- **Horoscopes/Astrological signs** (Aries, Taurus, Leo, etc.): Dabbling in this hobby opens one up to this spirit.

- **Phrenologist**: One who is supposed to foretell your future by the shape of your head.

- **Tarot cards**.

- **Ouija board**.

- **Pendulum**.

- **Dream interpreter**. (Any other than the Holy Spirit interpretation is evil.)

- **Household gods**, **idols**, **statues**, **pictures** or **drawings of spirit guides**, and **Buddha statues**. Also candles (as in lighting one for a prayer request in a church). Candles on a birthday cake also have a history. They date back to an ancient custom of burning a candle to a god for every year of your life to ward off evil spirits!

- **Talisman/good luck charm**s. (The word *luck* comes from the heathen god called Malukky.) A rabbit's foot, an amulet, or trinket that is supposed to possess magical powers. Animal skins in bracelet form or a headband (African culture); or a cross worn allegedly to ward off any evil.

- **The repetitive reciting of a magic verse or soun**d.

- **Effigies** (**voodooism**). Pins are stuck into effigies (doll images) with the intention of causing bodily harm to another person.

Many who are in an advanced stage of witchcraft, whether knowingly or unknowingly, often develop a muttering spirit. This manifests itself by gibbering away incoherently, while the person it is manifesting through, is seemingly unconscious that he or she has spoken at all.

Those who are possessed of a familiar spirit usually call it a personal *spirit guide...their household god!* This guide is theoretically on friendly and intimate terms with the person it possesses. This is evil.

Familiar spirits like to stay in families and will pass down through the generations. If your parents or grandparents dabbled in any of the foregoing, it is necessary to break all spiritual ties with this the most foul of spirits. God is both able and willing to set all free who call on Him.

No Christian should have a spirit guide other than the Holy Spirit. Go before the Lord, acknowledge your sin, and repent for your own protection, for it is abhorrence unto the Lord.

A warning: Children left to watch so-called "children's programs" on television should be monitored. Satan likes to seduce mankind as early in their lives as possible. Some programs using gods, supernatural beings, tarot cards, crystal balls, wizards, witches, and demons are used for indoctrination at an early age. These same children become very prone in later life to seek supernatural experiences and cults, after being programmed by uncensored television or films of weird supernatural beings doing good! Harry Potter is an example.

Up until seven years old, a child is being molded; and what is programmed into his spirit is what will establish itself as an adult. If you allow supernatural *rubbish in*, you can expect supernatural *rubbish out*!

SPIRIT OF WHOREDOM

My people ask counsel at their stocks [idols made of wood], *and their staff* [sticks or rods used for divination] *declareth unto them: for the spirit of whoredoms hath caused them to err* [to be deceived, go into error], *and they have gone a-whoring from under their God* (Hosea 4:12).

Manifestations

+ **Pornography**.

+ **Spiritual adultery**, consorting with "other gods."

+ **Lewdness** (see Ezek. 23:35).

+ **Idol worship** (see Ezek. 6:9).

+ **Fornication** and **adultery**; sexual sin of every kind (see Prov. 6:32).

+ **Love of social position** (see Matt. 23:6).

+ **Love of the world** (see 2 Tim. 4:10).

+ **Exhibition of the bod**y: strippers, lap dance girls, pole dancing, drag artists, streakers, cross dressers.

+ **Love of the body**: lewd pictures of the body, pornography, sexual perversion.

+ **Nudity**: naturism.

+ **Love of food**, unnaturally so (see Rom. 16:18; Phil. 3:19).

+ **Love of money**, unnaturally so (see 1 Tim. 6:10).

+ **Transvestites**.

+ **Pedophiles**.

+ **Prostitution**.

The world is forever searching for spiritual things and miraculous signs, and will continue to do so. Many will go into deception and satan worship. This is the spirit of whoredoms that tries to pervert and overrun the earth.

In the Book of Revelation, Babylon is called the *"mother of harlots and abominations of the earth."* These are people who will be deceived and go into perversion and false religions in the last days (see Rev. 17:5).

And he cried mightily with a strong voice, saying, Babylon the great is fallen, is fallen, and is become the habitation of devils, and the hold of every foul spirit, and a cage of every unclean and hateful

*bird. For all nations have drunk of the wine of the wrath of her for-
nication, and the kings of the earth have committed fornication
with her, and the merchants of the earth are waxed rich through
the abundance of her delicacies* (Revelation 18:2-3).

An important warning: Many people in witchcraft or satanism end
their lives in suicide or horrific deaths by their contemporaries, if they
try to leave. It is emphasized to initiates that no one is allowed to
leave a coven; they will kill you rather than let you go.

JESUS is the only one who can set you free, after an earnest repen-
tance, and a complete dependence on the power of Jesus Christ. At-
tempts might be made on your life, but He will sustain you and protect
you (see Ps. 91).

Get yourself into a fellowship that knows of your background and
of your decision for Christ. Explain to them your circumstances and
let them hold you constantly before the Lord in their prayers. With
their help and the power of Jesus Christ, you can overcome all attacks
from the foe.

Jesus said:

*All that the Father giveth me shall come to me; and him that
cometh to Me I will in no wise cast out* (John 6:37).

SPIRIT OF ERROR

*We are of God: he that knoweth God heareth us; he that is not of
God heareth not us. Hereby know we the spirit of truth, and the
spirit of error* (1 John 4:6).

Manifestations

◆ **Unable to confess Jesus Christ as the Son of God**.

◆ **Worldly**.

◆ **Spiritual deafness and dumbness**.

◆ **Religious spirit** (see 1 Tim. 4:2-3).

◆ **Seducing spirits** (cults); spiritually (see 1 Tim. 4:1).

- **Apostasy** (see 2 Tim. 2:16-18).

- **Atheism** (see 2 Tim. 2:16-18).

- **Unteachable spirit**.

- **Doctrine of devils** (see 1 Tim. 4:1).

- **Lies** (see 1 Tim. 4:2).

- **Idolatry** (see Gal. 5:20).

- **Sedition** (see Gal. 5:20).

- **Heresies** (see Gal. 5:20).

- **False teachings**.

SPIRIT OF INFIRMITY

And behold, there was a woman which had a spirit of infirmity eighteen years, and was bowed together, and could in no wise lift up herself (Luke 13:11).

Manifestations

- **Hunchback** (see Luke 13:11).

- **A deep-seated physical disorder** (see John 5:5).

- **Frailty**.

- **Weakness**.

- **Fever** (see Mark 1:30).

- **Boils** (see Exod. 9:9).

- **Leprosy** (see 2 Chron. 26:19).

- **Consumption** (see Lev. 26:16).

- **Dropsy** (see Luke 14:2).

- **Hemorrhoids** (see Deut. 28:27).

- **Asthma, hay fever**, and **sinus problems**.

- **Fungus**.

- **Allergies**.

- **Cancer/Leukemia**.

- **Bone disease**.

- **Lunacy**; all mental sicknesses.

- **Tumors**.

And His fame went throughout all Syria: and they brought unto Him all sick people that were taken with divers diseases and torments, and those which were possessed with devils, and those which were lunatic, and those that had the palsy; and He healed them (Matthew 4:24).

SPIRIT OF FEAR

For God hath not given us the spirit of fear; but of power, and of love, and of a sound mind (2 Timothy 1:7).

Manifestations

- **Asthma**.

- **Fear of animals** (abnormal).

- **Cowardice** (abnormal).

- **Ulcers of the stomach** (through unnatural worry, stress, and anxiety. Sometimes ulcers can be caused through abrasive medications, etc.; this is not the same thing).

- **Worry**; apprehension; anxiety (abnormal).

- **Dread** (see Exod. 15:16).

- **Nightmares** (see Ps. 91:5).

- **Afraid of the unknown** (abnormal) (see Ps. 91:6).

- **Fear of man** (abnormal) (see Isa. 51:12).

- **Fear of death** (see Heb. 2:14-15).

- **Heart attacks** (see Luke 21:26).

- **Stuttering.**

- **Insecurity** (see Deut. 28:66).

- **Torment** (see 1 John 4:18).

- **Inferiority; inadequacy; covers it up by belittling others**.

- **Terror; horror.**

- **Trembling** (see Ps. 55:5).

- **Phobias**: lifts, heights, the dark, germs, open spaces, washing hands or bathing many times per day, touching every lamppost, etc.).

- **Multiple personality disorder.**

- **Agitation.**

- **Timidity, undue caution, indecisive.**

- **Poverty.**

- **Murder** (see 1 Sam. 16:15-17).

- **Hatred** (see 1 Sam. 16:15-17).

- **Melancholy** (see 1 Sam. 16:15-17).

- **Undue fear of the devil** (see 2 Kings 17:35,37).

- **Blasphemy, foul mouth.**

- **Critical.**

- **Memory and thought-snatching** (not the natural aging process).

- **Rape** and **violence** can let in this spirit.

- **Child abuse** can let in this spirit.

- **Incest** can let in this spirit.

A person with an advanced form of *fear* cannot look another person in the eyes, but keeps their eyes averted.

Note: The spirit of fear is not to be confused with a *natural* fear given to us by the Lord for survival; i.e. not to stand on the edge of a cliff because we might fall; not to walk straight into traffic; and not to touch exposed electric cables; etc. These are normal self-preservation fears.

> *But the fearful, and unbelieving, and the abominable, and murderers, and whoremongers, and sorcerers, and idolaters, and all liars, shall have their part in the lake which burneth with fire and brimstone: which is the second death* (Revelation 21:8).

SPIRIT OF SLUMBER/STUPOR

> *According as it is written, God hath given them the spirit of slumber, eyes that they should not see, and ears that they should not hear; unto this day* (Romans 11:8).

God does not put an evil spirit on anyone. This Scripture states that according to man's behavior, man can come out from *under God's protection*, and therefore, leave himself open to this spirit.

Manifestations

- **Sleep**, unnatural sleep, especially at church meetings. (This is not referring to the elderly who sleep more and more as they age, which is natural.)

- **Listlessness**; undue listlessness.

- **Weariness**; undue weariness.

- **Inability to complete a project** or to work for long periods of concentration.

- **Daydreaming**; abnormal daydreaming.

- **Slothfulness** (see Prov. 26:13-16).

- **Idleness** (see Prov. 19:15).

- **Laziness** (see Prov. 19:15).

- **Poverty** (see Prov. 19:15; 6:11).

- **Sluggard** (see Prov. 26:16; 6:6-11).

- **Spiritually deaf and blind**; cannot receive the things of God.

- **Inertia**.

- **Lethargy**; abnormal lethargy.

- **Dazed for no reason**.

- **Passivity** (unusually so).

- **Snatches thoughts and memories** (not because of the natural aging process).

All of the above in an abnormal, unnatural intensity.

SPIRIT OF PRIDE

Pride goeth before destruction, and an haughty spirit before a fall. Better it is to be of an humble spirit with the lowly, than to divide the spoil with the proud (Proverbs 16:18-19).

Manifestations

- **Haughty**.

- **Lofty looks** (see Jer. 48:29; Isa. 2:11; 5:15).

- **Wrathful** (see Prov. 21:24).

- **Egotistical** (see 1 Cor. 4:18).

- **Boasting/braggart** (see 1 Pet. 5:5).

- **Stubborn/obstinate** (see Prov. 29:1).

- **Arrogant** (see 1 Pet. 5:3,5).

- **Vanity**; obsessed with oneself (see 1 Cor. 4:18).

- **Contentious** (see Prov. 13:10).

- **Self-righteous**; holier-than-thou attitude (see 1 Cor. 4:18; John 8:33,39).

- **Mockery/scornful** (see Prov. 3:34).

- **Disdain/supercilious**.

- **Condemning others**.

- **Anger**.

- **Domineering/overbearing** (see 1 Pet. 5:3,5).

- **Division/strife** (in home, work, or church place).

- **Superiority**; the feeling of grandeur (see Prov. 3:32).

- **Rudeness**.

- **Priggish**; overparticular about manners or speech, etc.

- **Unforgiveness**.

The ultimate condition of this spirit is to rob you of all authority and power as it did with satan. This spirit works well with *rebellion* and *witchcraft*.

DUMB AND DEAF SPIRIT

And they brought him unto Him [Jesus]*: and when he* [the spirit] *saw Him* [Jesus]*, straightway the spirit tare him; and he fell on the ground, and wallowed foaming. And He asked his father, How long is it ago since this came unto him? And he said, Of a child. And oftimes it hath cast him into the fire, and into the waters, to destroy him: but if thou canst do any thing, have compassion on us, and help us* (Mark 9:20-22).

When Jesus saw that the people came running together, He rebuked the foul spirit, saying unto him, Thou dumb and deaf spirit, I charge thee, come out of him, and enter no more into him. And the spirit cried, and rent him sore, and came out of him: and he was as one dead... (Mark 9:25-26).

Manifestations

- **Dumbness** (see Mark 9:17,25).

- **Foaming at the mouth** (see Mark 9:18,20).

- **Gnashing of teeth** (see Mark 9:18).

- **Pining away**, abnormal mourning, grief (see Mark 9:18,26).

- **Prostrations**, throwing down or laying flat, debilitate (see Mark 9:20).

- **Suicidal tendencies** (see Mark 9:22).

- **Deafness** (see Mark 9:22).

- **Teareth**, convulsions (see Mark 9:25,27).

- **Screaming** (see Mark 9:26).

- **Epilepsy** (see Mark 9:20).

- **Lunatic, insanity, madness, moonstruck.**

Lord, have mercy on my son: for he is lunatic, and sore vexed: for oft-times he falleth into the fire, and oft into the water (Matthew 17:15).

And, lo, a spirit taketh him, and he suddenly crieth out; and it teareth him that he foameth again, and bruising him... (Luke 9:39, see also verse 42).

Demons operate during *full moon* to make one think that it is the moon that causes the illness of insanity. In mental asylums, it is usually chaos around the time of a full moon.

- **Torment.**

- **Burns.**

- **Scalds.**

- **Bruising.**

- **Fainting.**

- **Blindness** (see Matt. 12:22).

- **Mute** (see Matt. 12:22).

This dumb and deaf spirit causes such heaviness of spirit that it lets in...

- **Sorrow** (see Prov. 14:13; 15:13).

- **A troubled spirit**.

- **Hopelessness**.

- **Self-pity**.

- **Loneliness** (feeling abnormally isolated).

- **Feebleness** (weak).

- **Faint**.

- **Depression** (leading to all manner of mental illness and nervous complaints).

- **Exhaustion** (physically and mentally).

Leading ultimately to...

- **Passivity**.

- **Suicide**.

- **Death**.

HEAVINESS

There is no such thing as an evil spirit of *heaviness*. You cannot get relief by casting out a demon. It's your own choice in allowing your spirit to become heavy. The Bible does not tell you to cast it out; it says, *"The oil of joy for mourning, the garment of praise for the spirit of heaviness..."* (Isa. 61:3b).

It's true that the devil can so beset you that you feel the heaviness seeping right down into your spirit. But when that happens, start *praising and rejoicing in the Lord*; consequently, the heaviness will depart.

Acting on God's Word and praising Him may seem difficult to do at the time, but try reading the Psalms out loud, mainly Psalm 138 through Psalm 150. Read and recite to the end of the Psalms, and before you know it, you will be dancing before Him. Heaviness will have flown away on the wings of praise to Almighty God, and joy will have replaced the heaviness. Christians have no right to be depressed; we should be brimming over with joy.

Jerry Savelle had a good way of advocating *joy*. This is what he said:

- The joy of the Lord is my strength.

- If I've no strength, then I am weak.

- If I am weak, I can't resist.

- If I can't resist, then the enemy can win.

- And if he's winning, then I'm not an overcomer!

SPIRIT OF LYING

Ye are of your father the devil, and the lusts of your father ye will do. He was a murderer from the beginning, and abode not in the truth, because there is no truth in him. When he speaketh a lie, he speaketh of his own: for he is a liar, and the father of it (John 8:44).

Manifestations

- **Idle words/flattery** (see 1 Tim. 6:20-21).

- **Hypocrisy**: Enlarges on the truth, or pretends a part, especially religion.

- **Religious**: For the world to see. No depth. Likes others to regard them as "holy."

- **Santa/Father Christmas**: Refers to a wealthy landowner called Nicolas, who lived in Europe. He was given sainthood by the Catholic Church and became St. Nicolas. Every Christmas he handed out food and presents to the poor. This is how the lie started. How can we lie to our children about the real meaning of Christmas? Christ...holiday. Or Christ...Mass is a time to celebrate the birth of our Savior, Jesus Christ; and the presents we give represents the gifts given to Jesus at His birth.

- **Easter Bunny/Easter eggs**: Ashtoreth (shortened Ishtar, shortened again to Easter) is a female god of Philistia and Zidon. She is supposed to be the wife of baal, and the queen of heaven.

The children gather wood, and the fathers kindle the fire, and the women knead their dough, to make cakes to the queen of heaven [hot cross buns!] (Jeremiah 7:18a).

Also read Jeremiah 44:18-27. Women made little cakes and drink offerings for the temple of Ashtoreth. Most often the temple priests were men in women's clothing, and prostitute devotees were there for the use of the priests. Orgies formed the main part of this pagan worship, and fertility rites were also performed. Fertility was represented by eggs, and rabbits are known for their rapid reproduction; hence, the peculiar habit of "Easter eggs" and "Easter bunnies" came about! In fact, on the Christian calendar, Easter is the time of the resurrection of our Lord Jesus, so why not give a little gift to celebrate "Happy Resurrection" day; but keep away from little cakes, bunnies, and Easter eggs. And tell your children the truth.

- **Tooth fairy** (see 1 Tim. 4:7).

- **Leprechaun** (see 1 Tim. 4:7).

- **Elf** (see 1 Tim. 4:7).

- **Imps** (see 1 Tim. 4:7).

- **Fairies** (see 1 Tim. 4:7).

- **Lies.**

- **Deception.**

- **False prophesy.**

- **All forms of superstition.**

  - **Black cat crossing in front of you.**

  - **Spilt salt**—the need to throw some over your shoulder.

  - **Breaking a mirror**—seven years of bad luck!

  - **Walking under a ladder.**

  - **Stepping on pavement cracks.**

  - **No blonde first over the threshold on New Years Day.**

➤ **Two spoons on a saucer supposedly means you will have twins.**

➤ **If you witness a bad accident while pregnant or are severely frightened, it will supposedly harm your baby!**

THE PERVERSE SPIRIT

The Lord hath mingled a perverse spirit in the midst thereof: and they have caused Egypt to err in every work thereof, as a drunken man staggereth in his vomit (Isaiah 19:14).

Manifestations

◆ **Evil speaking/backbiting/slander.**

◆ **Mischief** (see Prov. 17:20).

◆ **Pervert the way of judgment** (see Prov. 17:23).

◆ **Cause others to despise you** (see Prov. 12:8).

◆ **Cause a breach in the spirit** (see Prov. 15:4).

◆ **Impurity**; to think perverse things (see Prov. 23:33).

◆ **Carnal-minded** (see 1 Tim. 6:5).

◆ **Self-deception**; untruthful to self (see 1 Tim. 6:5).

◆ **Argumentative** (see 1 Tim. 6:5).

◆ **Confusion.**

◆ **Double-minded.**

◆ **Deceitful tongue** (see Prov. 15:4).

◆ **Lying** (see Isa. 59:3).

For your hands are defiled with blood, and your fingers with iniquity; your lips have spoken lies, your tongue hath muttered perverseness (Isaiah 59:3).

SPIRIT OF ANTICHRIST

And every spirit that confesseth not that Jesus Christ is come in the flesh is not of God: and this is that spirit of antichrist (1 John 4:3a).

Manifestations

♦ **Against Christ**; opposes His doctrine, His sonship, His victory, and His virgin birth.

♦ **False cults and religions**; insisting that church members use self-righteousness or "works" as a form of getting into Heaven. Christ's sacrifice and atonement for sin does not enter into their theology. Or they change the Word of God (Bible) to suit the particular doctrine of their cult.

♦ **Blasphemies**: Against God and the Holy Spirit by attributing the works of the Holy Sprit to the devil.

♦ **Strife**: They cause strife amongst God's people with the aim of disrupting fellowship.

♦ **Humanism**: Teaches that God is within everyone, and everyone is at one with nature, and not that *God* is the *Creator* and *Lord*.

♦ **Inability to pray**.

♦ **False teachers** (see 1 Tim. 6:3; James 3:14-6).

♦ **Proud** (unteachable).

♦ **Ignorant** (deliberate stupidity of God).

♦ **Envious**.

♦ **Railings** (accusing others).

♦ **Evil surmising** (interfering and jumping to wrong conclusions about others).

♦ **Tamuz sign/the sign of the cross**: This sign originated in the East, and is still used today by the Eastern cults, as they join palm to palm and make the sign of the cross in front of them. Likewise, in some traditional religions, priests make the sign of the cross over their congregations. It is, in fact, the *Tamuz* sign and has nothing to do with the cross of Christ, as Eastern religions do not acknowledge the cross of Christ.

THE SPIRIT OF LUST

Forasmuch then as Christ hath suffered for us in the flesh, arm yourselves likewise with the same mind: for he that hath suffered in the flesh hath ceased from sin; that he no longer should live the rest of his time in the flesh to the lusts of men, but to the will of God. For the time past of our life may suffice us to have wrought the will of the Gentiles, when we walked in lasciviousness, lusts, excess of wine, revellings, banquetings, and abominable idolatries (1 Peter 4:1-3).

Manifestations

◆ **Homosexual; drag** (see Eph. 4:19).

◆ **Lesbianism** (see Eph. 4:19).

◆ **Gluttony**; uninhibited indulgence of appetite (see Eph. 4:19).

◆ **Covetousness** (see Eph. 5:3).

◆ **Adultery** (see Eph. 5:3).

◆ **Fornication** (see Eph. 5:3).

◆ **Nudism, naturism**.

◆ **Exhibitionism**; streakers, flashers, etc.

◆ **Incest**.

◆ **Prostitution**.

◆ **Pornography**; any films, books, photos, or live shows.

◆ **Avarice**.

◆ **Necrophilia**.

◆ **Transvestite**.

◆ **Bestiality**.

◆ **Masturbation**.

◆ **Lasciviousness** (see 1 Pet. 4:3; Eph. 4:19).

◆ **Pedophiles**; child molestation.

◆ **Rapists**.

◆ **Unclean thought**s; often, satan will put unclean thoughts into your mind, but these are to be rejected, with no harm done. *Encouraging* these thoughts can let in this spirit.

◆ **Alcoholism** (see 1 Pet. 4:3).

◆ **Drug addictions**.

◆ **Idols**; either in the sporting field or "pop stars," or anything that takes precedence over God.

Anyone indulging in these immoralities will reap a good harvest from satan, the originator of lusts.

For this ye know, that no whoremonger, nor unclean person, nor covetous man, who is an idolater, hath any inheritance in the kingdom of Christ and of God (Ephesians 5:5).

THE SPIRIT OF BONDAGE

For ye have not received the spirit of bondage again to fear; but ye have received the Spirit of adoption, whereby we cry, Abba, Father (Romans 8:15).

Stand fast therefore in the liberty wherewith Christ hath made us free, and be not entangled again with the yoke of bondage (Galatians 5:1).

The evil deeds of a wicked man ensnare him; the cords of his sin hold him fast (Proverbs 5:22 NIV).

Manifestations

◆ **Apostasy**.

- **Phobias**; abnormal fear of anything—can't leave your house, can't walk on pavement cracks, etc. Some believe everything is dirty, so they have to keep repeatedly washing their hands; or they must touch every tree, etc.

- **Addiction**: alcohol, food, cigarettes, drugs, sex.

- **Blindness and deafness towards the Gospel**, either willingly or deliberately rejecting the Gospel.

- **Greed**: food, finances, all areas.

- **The need for power**: To make achievements; unnatural need to get ahead; to be the biggest and the best.

- **Anguish** (see Exod. 6:9).

- **Deception**: Entering into false religions or cults, Wicca, Jim Jones, Waco, Moonies, etc. (see Gal. 2:4-5).

- **Fear of death**: Unnatural morbid curiosity with death (this spirit works well with fear).

- **TV games**; some can be very addictive, especially the virtual reality ones. Christian parents should censor them.

- **Under the domination of another** (see Exod. 2:23); this spirit usually cooperates with the spirit of witchcraft operating in another person to dominate. The one who *dominates* is operating the *spirit of witchcraft*. The one who is *being dominated* has a *spirit of bondage*.

- **Anorexia**; Starts with heavy dieting due to the fear of being overweight; dieting becomes an obsession. This fear of eating causes an inability to swallow food.

- **Bulimia**: A fixation with being thin, inducing vomiting after binging on food.

SPIRIT OF REBELLION

An evil man seeketh only rebellion: therefore a cruel messenger shall be sent against him (see Prov. 17:11).

Manifestations

- **Pride**, **self-esteem**, **self-importance** (see Rom. 1:30).

- **Self-righteousness** (see Job 32:1) (not by the atoning works of Jesus Christ).

- **Prestige** (see Gen. 3:5; Ezek. 28:11-17; 3 John 9; 1 Tim. 3:6).

- **Power** (see Lev. 26:19).

- **Riches**: putting one's trust in riches and not God; making money their god (see Ps. 39:6; Ezek. 28:5).

- **Beauty**: the abnormal adoration of beauty (see Ezek. 28:11,17).

- **Warlike**: aggressive (see 2 Chron. 26:16).

- **Vanity of life**: the vaunting of one's self, vain boastings (see Rom. 1:30; James 4:16).

- **Glorifying in sexual activity**; **promiscuousness** (see 1 John 2:15-16).

- **Selfishness** (see 2 Tim. 2: 2-13).

- **Boasters** (see 2 Tim. 3:2).

- **Blasphemers** (see 2 Tim. 3:2).

- **Disobedient to parents**, **headstrong**, **disrespectful** (see 2 Tim. 3:2; Rom. 1:30).

- **Unthankful**, **ungrateful** (see 2 Tim. 3:2; Luke 6:35).

- **Unholy**: no reverence (see 2 Tim. 3:2).

- **Sexual perverts**: without natural affection, homosexual, lesbian (see Rom. 1:31).

- **Truce breakers** (see 2 Tim. 3:2).

- **False accusers**, **slanderers**, **backbiting** (see 2 Tim. 3:3).

- **Incontinent**: no control of passions (see 2 Tim. 3:3).

- **Fierce**: wild, savage, and brutal (see 2 Tim. 3:3).

- **Despisers of good men**: dislike and ridicule them (see 2 Tim. 3:3).

- **Traitors**: betrayers, treacherous (see 2 Tim. 3:4).

- **Heady**: rash, reckless, headstrong (see 2 Tim. 3:4).

- **High-minded**: insensitive, conceited, silly behavior (see 2 Tim. 3:4).

- **Lovers of pleasure**: sensual, self-gratification (see 2 Tim. 3:4).

- **Piety**: zealously impressing others with their religiosity (see 2 Tim. 3:5). Godly piety never puts on a show.

- **Faithless**: opposes faith in others, ridicules the works of God (see 2 Tim. 3:5).

- **Resists truth**.

- **Self-deception**: of self, having itchy ears to hear what they want to hear, not necessarily the truth.

- **Deception leads others along the wrong path**.

- **Apostasy**.

This spirit usually works together with the spirit of rejection.

THE ROOT OF REBELLION

There is an aspect of rebellion that we must cover; this is from the parent's position.

Train up a child in the way he should go: and when he is old, he will not depart from it (Proverbs 22:6).

Note that rebellion nearly always has its roots in childhood. God places an awesome task upon parents to be responsible for the raising of their offspring. Parents are more often than not the ones to blame when their children go into rebellion. The task of being a parent is enormous, and the reason that there are so many broken homes and divorces today is simply the result of this spirit.

Knowing your child is on the wrong path of life, but not wanting to "rock the boat," or attempting to retain their friendship and hoping that they will "grow out of it" is the worst disservice you can do to your child. Believe me, when a child has no restrictions, he will definitely go into rebellion.

Then there is another type of parent who is always there to remind their child that he or she has done something wrong—and there are many occasions to do so. We use each situation to point out their shortcomings and faults. We even go as far as criticizing in the hope of showing them the "right way." We, of course, learned this mode of bringing up children from our own parents...and they from theirs!

God's Word says you must train up a child in *the way he should go*! This is vitally important. Just as the rest of God's Word has been given as a guide to us, so the phrasing of this verse is of the utmost importance.

In fact, what we are accomplishing by not adhering to this plan is building resentment into our children; no matter how great an achievement they have made, we are always expecting more of them. For the most part, it is because we want our children to succeed, be acceptable, and conform to the standards set by mankind, instead of God.

But the Word says, *"Train up a child in the way he **should go**"* (Prov. 22:6a). Let me give you a few examples.

Your son comes home from his favorite sports activity and announces, "Dad, I've just made the first team."

"Good," says the father. "Maybe next year you will make captain!"

The boy's best effort was not good enough for Dad! A seed of resentment takes root.

A mother arrives home to find the kitchen floor awash with water and her small daughter up to her elbows in soapsuds.

"Look, Mom. I've washed all the dishes for you!"

"Oh no, Jane! Just look at my floor! You've washed the dishes for me, but now you have left me with another job to do on the floor...and did you have to use so much dishwashing liquid?"

Jane's effort was not good enough for her mother—a seed of resentment starts to grow.

Lastly and most common...a three-year-old boy falls off his tricycle, and his five-year-old sister goes to pick him up. The mother yells, "Betty, what's wrong with you? I've told you before to watch your brother. Move out of my way while I clean him up, you naughty girl!" Resentment moves into the heart of little Betty.

What am I saying? Am I advocating that children be relieved of all duties and responsibilities in the household? No, I am not. But let us look at each of these situations again, the way God intended.

Your son has just announced that he has made the first team in a sports program. You say, "Son, that's great! I'm really proud of you. You deserve to make the team because you have put in a lot of hard practice. Man, let's go and tell your mother! You know, Billy, if you keep training as hard as you have, it wouldn't surprise me one day if you make captain."

The child will feel his efforts have been worthwhile, and the bond grows between father and son. The father complimented the child, *and then told him the way to go*!

If the mother arrived home to a wet kitchen floor and acted as God intended, she would have said to her daughter, "Oh, honey, I really appreciate all your help. It is very thoughtful of you. Are you going to help me wipe up the floor afterwards? Then the entire kitchen will be spotless. I don't think it will be necessary to use as much suds next time though, because you look as if you are having a bubble bath!" Both females would have finished up in giggles and an extra effort on the little girl's part would be made next time, in trying again to please Mommy.

As far as the last illustration is concerned, the first thing that parents must learn is that *both* children are *their* responsibility. The responsibility of the younger child should never be placed into the hands of a child who is older. The older child is incapable of giving the younger one the expert attention that parents could and should give him.

The older child has a right to a childhood of her own, and taking care of someone junior to her is *robbing* her of that right. However, Mom is not a super being either, who is able to give the children her undivided attention all day. And sometimes—*not all the time*—a little help from an older child can be useful.

But if little Johnny falls off his tricycle while his sister is supposed to be keeping an eye on him, then Mom should simply pick up the little boy and say, "Oh, Betty, I wish you had been watching over him properly. But I know you don't like to see him cry either, so, Betty, you pick up the tricycle, and let's take him inside and wash him up." The little girl will realize her mistake and will try a little harder next time.

One more "never" for our list is: *Never* chastise or punish a child in front of other people as this humiliates and belittles him, making him feel inferior—not only compounding resentment but leaving him with rejection and a very poor self-image that he carries into adulthood. He will have a tendency to copy the example by bad-mouthing his peers; and later, if he marries, he will continue this humiliation with his own children.

Resentment leads to *bitterness*, and bitterness leads to *rebellion*.

A child who feels resentment ultimately feels anger and rebellion towards his parents, his school, and towards authority of any kind and ultimately towards God. This type of person is inevitably the one who rebels against any restriction in marriage and is often found in the divorce courts!

God has placed into parents' hands the shaping of the future generation. Bring that generation up according to God's Word, and a godly, upright generation should be the result.

Remember, parents, a phrase well worth repeating: *Authority* without compassion is called *oppression*.

SPIRIT OF REJECTION

This is one of the most active spirits and can even be given entry while the child is still *in the womb* by parents who:

- ▸ Do not want a child.

- ▸ Reject a sickly child.

- ▸ Reject an unlovely child.

- ‣ Reject a difficult child.

- ‣ Reject an abnormal child.

Manifestations

- ◆ **Inadequacy**.

- ◆ **Lack of self-confidence**.

- ◆ **Unable to be positive**.

- ◆ **Aggressive**.

- ◆ **Sarcasm**; caustic tongue.

- ◆ **Low self-image**; having no worth in their own eyes.

- ◆ **Self-pity**.

- ◆ **Inferiority**.

- ◆ **Wavering**; double-minded.

- ◆ **Martyred**.

- ◆ **Unstable in relationships with the opposite sex**.

- ◆ **Introvert**: an advanced form of rejection.

- ◆ **Resentment**.

- ◆ **Bitterness**.

- ◆ **Tends to put oneself under a dominant figure**.

- ◆ **Rejection of self**; suicide.

- ◆ **Cannot accept the love of others or God towards them**.

- ◆ **Depression**.

- ◆ **Insecurity**.

- ◆ **Guilt**.

This spirit has a two-fold way of working. The spirit of rejection hovers over a person and torments him by oppression, *causing those around him to reject him*. This oppression causes others to feel angry, hateful, or disapproving towards him; and nothing he says or does seems right to them. They mentally push him away and reject him. He, in turn, feels the rejection and as a defense rejects them. A *spirit of rejection* never enters a person until an outside force has first rejected him. Over a period of time, he gives entry to a *spirit of rejection* and rejects the world at large.

WALLS BUILT UP BY REJECTION AND REBELLION

The ultimate state of rebellion is murder. The ultimate state of rejection is suicide.

Rejection is worked on a pendulum with *rebellion*. When the host feels rejection, his mood swings straight into rebellion, and then guilt

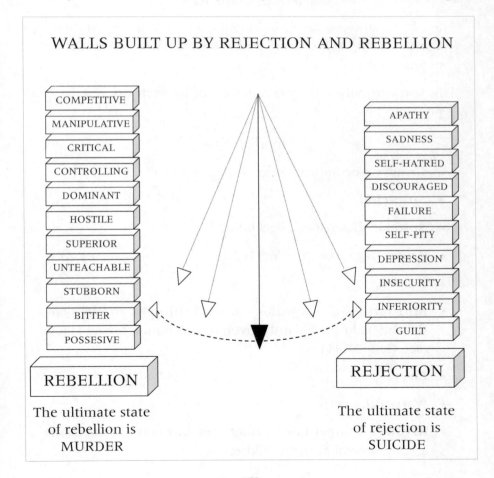

WALLS BUILT UP BY REJECTION AND REBELLION

COMPETITIVE
MANIPULATIVE
CRITICAL
CONTROLLING
DOMINANT
HOSTILE
SUPERIOR
UNTEACHABLE
STUBBORN
BITTER
POSSESIVE

REBELLION

APATHY
SADNESS
SELF-HATRED
DISCOURAGED
FAILURE
SELF-PITY
DEPRESSION
INSECURITY
INFERIORITY
GUILT

REJECTION

The ultimate state
of rebellion is
MURDER

The ultimate state
of rejection is
SUICIDE

causes him to swing back into rejection, of self and others. *These two spirits work well together.* A person who has a spirit of rejection finds it difficult to give or receive love naturally.

Before any deliverance is possible, this person has to *forgive* those who have rejected him; and after deliverance, it is important that he has prayer for *inner healing.* Usually, there are many areas that need God's salve applied, including the restoration of a good self-image and self-worth.

The person with a spirit of rejection is usually very prickly and unloving, but the reward of seeing them set free and being able to express love for the first time is well worth the effort.

SPIRIT OF JEALOUSY

> *For love is strong as death; jealousy is cruel as the grave: the coals thereof are coals of fire, which hath a most vehement flame* (Song of Solomon 8:6b).

This spirit usually torments a person of low self-esteem, an insecure person.

Manifestations

- **Cruelty** (see Song of Solomon 8:6).

- **Suspicion**.

- **Spite**: maliciousness, backbiting.

- **Anger**: rage (see Prov. 6:34).

- **Hatred**.

- **Murder**: Esau was jealous of the birthright and blessing that he had nonchalantly given to Jacob for a bowl of stew (see Gen. 27:41).

- **Envy**.

- **Watchful**: overly.

- **Rivalry**: competition, sometimes promoted by parents among several of their children.

- **Selfish**: self-absorbed.

- **Aggressive**.

- **Coveting**: "keeping up with the Jones's"; one-upmanship towards others.

- **Disunity**: of home, or church or workplace.

- **Delusion**: believing that their suspicions are always justified.

- **Critical spirit**.

11

THE CHRISTIAN OBJECTIVE

By now, you will have realized that if we are to maintain some form of control in our lives, a decision has to be made. We cannot fight against the evil that exists in the world without taking a stand. Whether we like it or not, satan is still alive and thriving on the earth! And while men live on this planet, his agenda is to torment and destroy mankind. That is a fact. Every family on earth has been touched at one time or another with satan's evil tentacles. We have to realize that we are not able to stand against this old master of evil all on our own.

It seems that only God Almighty has the ability to fight and conquer this archenemy. Therefore, the question we need to answer is: Will we continue to let the devil play havoc with our lives and try to withstand the blows and heartache he brings, or will we throw in our lot with God? Accept the sacrifice of Jesus Christ who died for mankind's sins and reconciliation with God. Then get yourself tucked into the glorious army that God is putting together. For with or without us, God *will be the victor*. He doesn't need you, but you need Him if you are to survive this planet unscathed!

All power and fulfillment can be found in Jesus Christ. Satan is only a created being and is in no way equal in power or authority to Jesus Christ. Read the Bible from Genesis to Revelation—Christ wins! If satan is so great, why does he not rule Heaven? Is it because he himself has been barred from Heaven by a force superior to himself? Nowhere in the Bible does it say that satan will someday rule Heaven together with Almighty God...so why follow a loser? What can a created being, just like us, offer mankind? Satan knows his ultimate abode is the lake of fire; so, does it make sense to follow a being who can only offer you a place next to him in an eternal fire? Every person born on this planet has to decide if he will follow the loser (satan) or follow God. And no fence-sitters are allowed; you *must* choose one or the other...there is no alternative. God or satan?

Until you get to the point where you are prepared to pay any cost for spiritual freedom, you won't fight for it. God's plan for you was never to just get by, or have just enough money, or be subjected to any crime or mishap that might come your way, or accept sickness in your body. In fact, it was never God's intention that you simply not make waves or just accept each day as it comes.

He wants you to live a victorious life. He has made provision for you to live a life of plenty, a healthy life, a secure life. If you are not living like that, then you are living below God's intended lifestyle for you. And the only way to achieve this secure lifestyle is to be prepared to fight for it.

What you achieve in your lifetime is only by natural talent and ability; it is what you can achieve over and above your best efforts that will take faith, and living in faith is what God requires of us. The price of living in God's intended lifestyle is to do spiritual warfare, to take back from satan what he has stolen from you, and to prevent him from taking anything else from you. The devil is your archenemy, and he has made it his life's work to keep each person living far below the lifestyle God Almighty ordained for him. Hence, you have a choice to make; either stay in your comfort zone and accept what the world throws at you, or rise up, become part of God's glorious army, and fight in the spiritual realm for what is legally yours—a carefree life.

Spiritual freedom fighters have a price to pay. It takes stamina and a thorough knowledge of who God is, what Christ did for mankind, along with the ongoing power of the Holy Spirit, and the knowledge of the satanic realm and tactics. It also takes guts to stride out in faith and become an overcomer to achieve the way of life that God intended, with each person winning the race God has set before us. Choose the winning side; accept Jesus Christ's atonement for your sin and join the glorious army.

It is essential that believers rise up and take on the role for which they were created and destined. Every member of the Church is able to become a part of God's glorious end-time army. We have a duty to our Savior to enlist and become a radical sword-bearing overcomer…then the gates of hell will not prevail! Every blood-washed child of God is obligated to be part of the glorious army that Jesus is coming back for.

THE OVERCOMER

In order for evangelizing, teaching, preaching, miracles, and the laying on of hands and other ministries to be effective in the Church, it is essential that prayer warriors first do battle in the heavenlies so that they can pull down any principalities or powers that hinder these ministries and open up the way for the powerful moving of the Holy Spirit. This ministry is vital in the scheme of an orderly running church. In other words, having the ability to do effective spiritual warfare prayer becomes the backbone for all other ministries.

It never fails to amaze me how many rewards are offered in the Book of Revelation for being an overcomer. God obviously considers this a high priority.

> *For whatsoever is born of God overcometh the world: and this is the victory that **overcometh** the world, even our faith. Who is he that overcometh the world, but he that believeth that Jesus is the Son of God?* (1 John 5:4-5)

> *He that hath an ear, let him hear what the Spirit saith unto the churches; To him that **overcometh** will I give to eat of the tree of life, which is in the midst of the paradise of God* (Revelation 2:7).

*He that hath an ear, let him hear what the Spirit saith unto the churches; To him that **overcometh** will I give to eat of the hidden manna, and will give him a white stone, and in the stone a new name written, which no man knoweth saving he that receiveth it* (Revelation 2:17).

*And he that **overcometh**, and keepeth My works unto the end, to him will I give power over the nations* (Revelation 2:26).

*He that **overcometh**, the same shall be clothed in white raiment; and I will not blot out his name out of the book of life, but I will confess his name before My Father, and before His angels* (Revelation 3:5).

*Him that **overcometh** will I make a pillar in the temple of my God, and he shall go no more out: and I will write upon him the name of my God, and the name of the city of my God, which is new Jerusalem, which cometh down out of heaven from my God: and I will write upon him My new name* (Revelation 3:12).

*To him that **overcometh** will I grant to sit with Me in My throne, even as I also overcame, and am set down with My Father in His throne* (Revelation 3:21).

*He that **overcometh** shall inherit all things; and I will be his God, and he shall be My son* (Revelation 21:7).

God Himself must have the last word on the subject of overcomers...

No man that warreth entangleth himself with the affairs of this life; that he may please him who hath chosen him to be a soldier (2 Timothy 2:4).

This charge I commit unto thee...according to the prophecies which went before on thee, that thou by them mightest war a good warfare (1 Timothy 1:18).

And finally...in Isaiah 54:16b-17 (NIV):

"And it is I who have created the destroyer [satan] *to work havoc; no weapon forged against you will prevail, and you will refute every tongue that accuses you. This is the heritage of the servants of the Lord* [the believer], *and this is their vindication from Me,"* declares the Lord.

DAILY COVERING PRAYER

I have always found that in the spiritual realm, attack is the best form of defense; therefore, I use this covering prayer each day, which goes a long way to protect one's self and all that one holds dear.

Declaration of love to…God the Father, the God of Abraham, Isaac, Jacob, and [insert your own name]; the Lord Jesus Christ, the Living Word made flesh and dwelt amongst us, Son of God, Savior; the Holy Spirit, my teacher, comforter, and guide.

I acknowledge…Your Godhead in complete unity with Your Word and Your Holy Spirit. In faith, I give license to be used by You for any purpose You desire.

I reject…all evil in thought, word, or deed. I reject satan and all his works and every evil force that tries to influence my mind, body, soul, or spirit.

In thanksgiving…for Your love, Word, grace, peace, prosperity, protection, purpose, joy, perfect health, wisdom, understanding, and all spiritual gifts. You, Father, are in full control of my life. For my sound mind and senses to appreciate all Your beauty and grace. For the family that You blessed me with, including their loved ones and Your promise to me that "Me and my household would be saved, and my sons and daughters would prophesy." For this new day and all Your beauty that I see in all You created in nature around me. For the very air that I breathe and for the blessings that overtake me according to Your Word (see Deut. 28).

Forgiveness…I repent of [name your sin], and I ask for Your forgiveness. I forgive all who have hurt me [name them]. I choose to forgive of my own free will.

Protection (see Isa. 54:17)…I claim immunity against evil, including the evil of the spoken work and declare before You: *No evil shall prosper that is formed against me, but shall return void; that when the enemy comes against me in one direction, You will scatter him in seven directions.* I claim this promise on behalf of myself and my children unto all generations including their loved ones, our goods, finances, animals, vehicles, businesses, workplaces, our relationships and marriages, and in all other things in which You have blessed and prospered us in.

I declare before You, Father, that satan has no dominion over any member of my family or myself, physically, mentally, spiritually, socially, or financially. According to Your Word, I condemn every evil word or curse that has or will be directed at my family or myself and our possessions, businesses, finances, relationships or animals—even if the word or curse goes forth unintentionally. Every evil word or curse shall return void and will not accomplish that whereunto it was sent.

I stand against, according to your Word, principalities, powers, spiritual wickedness in high places, satan and demon spirits; and render them harmless, powerless, and ineffective against myself and my family. *In the name of Jesus Christ*, no evil formed against us can prosper, for greater is He who is in me than he who is in the world. I know, Father, that You have set a hedge around every believer, and I acknowledge this. I also believe Your Word, that You have given us angels to minister for us; therefore, I ask You to position warring angels around my property and land for complete protection. No evil force is allowed over the perimeter of my land so that the peace of God will reign supreme in my home.

I pull down the strongmen of violence, indifference, and stupor in this land so that peace will prevail here. I pray for the government, that the right people will be placed in power and that they rule wisely and justly. I pray for the armed forces, including the police force, that You will fill them with integrity and justice. I pray for universities, colleges, and schools, that the minds of our youth are taught of your ways and satan will not influence or control them. Lastly, I pray for all children everywhere, to be fully protected from abuse of any kind.

Armor (see Ephesians 6:11-18)…According to Your Word, I put on the whole armor with which You have provided me, for I know that we wrestle not against flesh and blood, but against the strategies and deceits of the devil. Therefore, I put on the *breastplate of righteousness*. I thank You that I am the righteousness of God in Jesus Christ. I thank You, Father, that my heart is guarded, and I allow the Word of Christ to dwell in me richly. My attitudes and emotions are guarded because of the breastplate of righteousness.

My feet are shod with the *shoes of peace*. I choose to put on my "go ye" shoes. I thank You for Your peace that passes all understanding. My footsteps are ordered of the Lord, and every place on which my foot shall tread You have given it to me. Satan, you are under my feet today, because I have been given authority to tread on serpents and scorpions and over all your power. I walk in total *victory*, and I choose to walk in *love* today.

I put on the *girdle of truth*. I know the *Truth* (Jesus), and the *Truth* shall set me free. Lead me in Your truth and teach me Your ways, oh Lord, for I worship You in Spirit and in Truth.

I take up my *sword of the Spirit*, which is the Word of God (Bible) that the Holy Spirit uses as a weapon against the foe. The Word of God is quick and powerful and sharper than any two-edged sword. I thank You for the power of Your Word, Father, that when we speak it, it becomes energized and breaks the power of the enemy. The Word of God shall not depart from out of my mouth. Teach me the mysteries of Your Word, Lord.

I take up my *shield of faith* that completely covers me and quenches every fiery dart sent by the wicked one. I choose to walk in faith and practice faith. My faith comes from hearing and hearing from the Word of God. Jesus is the author and finisher of my faith. In faith, I know that You watch over Your Word to perform it. I surround my family with faith and have confidence that You will watch over them and protect them in all their ways.

Lastly, I put on the *helmet of salvation* that also protects my mind, and I thank You that the Word renews my mind. I cast down every wicked and vain imagination that would rise itself up in my mind. I take my thoughts captive to the obedience of Christ Jesus. Thank You for my sound mind. I know I have the mind of Christ and hold the thoughts, feelings, and purposes of His heart. Holy Spirit, give direction to my spirit and illuminate my mind today.

I am now fully armed and above all circumstances today!

Restitution…

And He shall send Jesus Christ, which before was preached unto you: whom the heaven must receive until the times of restitution of all things, which God hath spoken by the mouth of all His holy prophets since the world began (Acts 3:20-21).

I now declare before you, satan, that according to this Scripture, I have a right to regain what you have stolen from me and have it restored immediately. This includes...[name what has been stolen, i.e., fellowship, joy, peace, relationships, etc.]. So, make restitution immediately, in multiple-fold, so that the Scriptures can be fulfilled.

Dedication...As I have accepted Christ as my Savior, I am now known by the name of "Christian." I yield my body, soul, and spirit to You, Father, and *pray the words of my mouth and the meditations of my heart* will be acceptable to You, so that I *will build up* and not break down, *heal* and not destroy, thereby bringing glory and honor to the name that I bare. Put a guard around my mouth today and give me great love for the brethren.

Sister Wisdom (see Proverbs 8)...I speak to sister wisdom. I am the apple of my Father's eye. I have His anointing upon me. I have abundance in my spiritual area and supernatural recall of the Word of God. I have all wisdom, understanding, and revelation of God's Word. I desire above all things to be full of God's wisdom.

I place my will under God's will today to do whatever He desires.

By faith...My body is and will stay perfect in all its functions; for I am set free from the curse of sin and sickness through Christ Jesus, and I know I am fearfully and wonderfully made in Your image.

I claim the same immunity from sin and sickness for all my family and their loved ones. I reject any foreign body, germ, or disease that would try to establish itself in my members, or that of my family, with intent to destroy or disfigure, therefore standing perfect as You, our God, created and intended us to be.

Now, beloved Father, I go through this day *fearing not*, believing in You; *standing still*, leaning on You; *holding my peace*, trusting in You; and *entering into Your rest*—all in the name of our Lord Jesus Christ.

12

A DEVILISH SCENARIO

Darkness covered the earth...

In the heavenly realms, an angel presented the blood of the cruci-fied Christ to the Father. Father God held out His hands to receive the blood, and as it dripped from the majestic fingers, the emotion of re-lief and triumph crossed His beautiful face.

A cry echoed down the corridors of Heaven, "The Blood avails, the Blood avails! The sacrificial Blood of Jesus Christ has been accepted by the Father, for the remission of mankind's sins. The Blood avails!"

The holy angels exalted the Father with praise and rejoicing. Singing reverberated through Heaven and permeated the throne room as a beautiful perfume. The heavenly hosts were jubilant, and their thunderous ecstatic cries were heard in the deep portals of the universe. The singing and fragrance of angelic praises even filtered through the rank, putrefying depths of hell.

Down below on the decaying, putrid floor of hell laid the body of Jesus, while the Holy Spirit stood close by. When the Spirit heard the rejoicing, an exquisite smile covered His face. He knelt and gently touched the lifeless, scarred body of Jesus!

Deep within His body a light began to shine, slowly permeating His entire being with brilliance and life. The energy force of the Father quickened His body. The Spirit of the Father pulsated through His members, radiating life. His eyes snapped open, and His bruised and broken body took on wholeness and perfection once more. *The Light of the world lived again!*

Jesus leapt to His feet; the Spirit and Jesus embraced and congratulated each other warmly, and then, humming a worship song, the Spirit left, turning just once to flash a cheeky grin at Jesus. "We did it!" Jesus checked the fetid hallways of hell for direction, then turned abruptly and marched towards the throne room where satan was holding court in all his pomp and evil majesty, celebrating the demise of God's only Son.

A black cloud of sin hung over the satanic throne. Satan had tried to imitate the splendors of Almighty God's Kingdom, but had failed miserably; and all the glitter and gold were just a cheap imitation, which seemed fitting somehow as so was he!

Every sin imaginable was being enacted in front of his satanic majesty. A cry of terror mixed with devilish screams set the high notes in a vibrato of evil chanting. Demons gyrated lewdly back and forth in a macabre dance before the devil and his angels. A malevolent smile creased the face of the devil as he looked over his subjects. The angels licked their lips in evil anticipated pleasure as every lurid sin was displayed before them. The smell of iniquity mixed with the putrefying smell of death swirled around the throne in a purple haze. From cracks in the stone floor, jets of sulphur burst forth in macabre accompaniment, to the gyrating dance of the demons.

All of a sudden, the urgent blood-curdling scream of a demon alerted them. The sickly pale faces of the fallen angels contorted in fear as they saw Jesus stride with authority into the satanic throne room.

The demons surrounding the throne shrank back in terror and scurried beneath satan's black cloak of death. The devil straightened his back in boldness, rising to his full impressive height, though he could not control the trembling that ran through his body at the sight of Jesus in His glorious resurrected body.

With calm confidence, Jesus walked right up to the devil's throne. Satan desperately tried not to cringe or pull away at the closeness of Christ, though the shaking of his body belied his bravado, and made his throne rattle. With an air of impudence, though his heart pounded in fear, the devil's face broke into a ghoulish satanic grin as he tried to stare down the risen Christ.

Returning his gruesome smile with a sweet smile of His own, Jesus said, "Relax, devil, I'm not here to bind you or throw you into the lake of fire at this time."

Not wanting his subjects to see his terror and relief, the devil snapped back, "You don't frighten me, Jesus. You are finished. I have destroyed You; You are dead! You have no power here, for this is *my kingdom*. So what do You want? Do You want to join us?"

Ignoring his jibe, Jesus looked directly at the keys hanging from satan's belt. "Where did you get them?" He asked, pointing to the keys. The devil's hand covered the keys on his belt, the cold hard metal reassuring him of his control. He glared at Jesus in defiance.

The demons restlessly ducked and dived beneath the devil's full-length, mildewed robe, feeling secure in his presence. Their malevolent eyes glowed and their satirical smiles showed rotted teeth as they leered at the Lord Jesus through the holes in the devil's cloak. They gave off an acrid stink, and the disgusting smell formed an eerie green vapor that floated around the throne room, like pulsating clouds of evil around the devil's head.

Apprehensively, the fallen angels crowded together, their pallid faces distorted with terror as they watched the devil push out his chest in pride. His eyes were mere slits, as triumph etched his face and wickedness emanated from his very being.

"Thousands of years ago a man called Adam had these keys. God gave them to him. They are the keys to this planet and to life, but Adam sinned against God and disobeyed Him." Satan chuckled as he remembered. "Adam had the keys of the earth and all in it. He also had the keys to life's blessings, to peace, love, joy, and fulfillment. In addition, he had the ability to fellowship with God every day. Among the keys, he also had the keys to death and hell—he had them all...and I took them away from him! He was so easy to deceive!" laughed the evil one. "He chose me. Do You hear that, Jesus? He chose to obey me, and I became his master instead of God. Every thing Adam owned became mine. Because the keys now legally belong to me, I have been running the earth, my way—because it is mine to run!" screeched the devil belligerently. He stomped around his throne, his head thrown back in vanity, and chest pushed out in pride, as he sought to impress his subjects and subdue Jesus.

"Well," said Jesus, in disdain, "have I got news for you. *I am the second Adam*! And I have paid the price for the first Adam's indiscretion. I gave My life on Calvary as a sacrifice for Adam's transgression, as indeed for all of mankind's sin. I have paid in full and am now claiming the legal right and authority to take back those keys. When sacrifice for sin was made on Calvary, ownership of the earth returned to Me. Those keys now belong to Me. Your days of ruling the earth are over!" He said in a voice that reverberated throughout the devil's kingdom.

Satan and his retinue screamed in horror and pain as they started to tremble and quiver. They pulled back in fear with a chorus of "Ah's," as Jesus took a step closer to satan. Christ frowned as the fetid smell of fear swirled around them and hit His nostrils.

Menacingly, Jesus brought His face up close to satan's ashen-gray face. "You've brought sickness and disease to the earth," Jesus said quietly as He controlled His anger. "I bring health." He stepped even closer to the devil and looked at him eyeball to eyeball. And as much as the devil tried, he couldn't pull away. The piercing eyes of the Son of God held him fast.

"You brought poverty into the world; I bring wealth. You brought condemnation and damnation; I bring absolute forgiveness. You brought sin; but I bring righteousness. You brought death; but I give eternal life. You've had your day, satan. Now the earth belongs to Me. You do not rule mankind anymore, so give Me back those keys!" Jesus demanded.

The devil fell backwards in fear as Jesus yanked the keys from the belt on his waist. Screams of terror erupted from the demons and reverberated around the throne room as they scurried from beneath the black robe. "Don't touch us. Keep away from us, leave us alone!" they yelled in horror.

"What are You going to do?" whimpered the devil, his sin-wrinkled face turning a shade of slimy green.

"I'm going to free the prisoners from this pit of hell. Those God-fearing patriarchs of old are going to be freed. Yes, you've guessed it; I am going to let out all the righteous captives that you have held in this terrible place for so long and set them free from your domain. You see, satan, you no longer have the power over life and death. From now on, it will be *absent from the body and present with the Lord* for My people, because I, the second Adam, have taken repossession of the earth and all the authority that goes with it when I defeated death. Never again will My creation have to spend time in this God-forsaken place. When they die, you no longer have a hold over them! It is I who now have *the keys*, and you will never again have any legal right to keep any blood-washed, sin-forgiven child of God in this place!"

Cocky as ever, the devil smirked, "Then what, Jesus? Do You really think mankind will realize that You now *own* the earth? Will everything now be peace and love? You think the abortions will stop, and the Christian truth will be taught in schools, and people will believe in God again? Will all sin vanish? Forget it! I did too good of a job there, and I will continue to delude and deceive every human being who gives me the right. I'll cause havoc and chaos in their lives...and You can't stop me!" he screamed.

"You're right. The Father and I will not take away man's free will. And if a man gives you permission, by following your ways, you have a legal right to torment him. But remember this, *I am the firstborn of many*. Those I left back on the earth, those who believe on My Word will be just like Me, and able to do the works I did. They will spread the word about you; they will hunt you and your followers down and cast you into outer darkness, just the same as I did. They will not stand for your evil ways. You will not rule them; they won't let you. And you won't be able to hide from them.

"Oh no!" screamed the demons. "He was bad enough when He walked the earth, but how will we withstand it if His followers multiply?"

"Exactly," said the Lord. "I've given them My name, and I've given them My authority and power. I've already told them that no evil formed against them can prosper. Using My name, nothing will stop them! You thought you had only Me to contend with, but those I placed My name upon, in the flesh, they will defeat you! They do not fear you. I bought back their right standing with God. I sacrificed My life for the forgiveness of their sins, but it is *their* faith, *their* willingness, and *their* fearlessness to fight you in the spiritual realm that will bring you down," Jesus said triumphantly.

Then His laughter echoed from ages past and through all eternity. He laughed as He strode triumphantly out of the throne room. "You're finished, satan...I win!"

As Jesus headed for the light, the devil screamed in panic, "Lock the doors of hell, and fortify the gates. If what He says is true, we have to barricade ourselves in!"

Amidst the confusion and chaos, the clear solitary voice of Jesus Christ echoed through the hallways of hell. "It won't do you any good, satan, *because the gates of hell will not prevail against My people!*"

He smiled as He strode into Father God's presence, the keys of death and hell dangling from His fingers...

THE DEVIL'S LAST SONG

Long ago I planned in my passing pride
That today I should reign as king.
But "Where is my kingdom? Where is my crown?"
Is the bitter song that I sing.

What joy have I won through my evil designs,
What peace in my soul-wrecking plan?
I hoped to conquer both Heaven and hell
But have won nothing more than mere man.

I can see o'er the bridgeless gulf
The glorified Heaven-lit strand.
My chains make me feel the double disgrace
As I crouch 'neath the Infinite Hand.

Where are my princes, my legions of dupes,
And the millions of souls I have won?
My pains and my chains are greater by far
Because of the deeds I have done.

All my plans and my schemes in a thousand ways
Like bubbles are blown out of sight.
My fancies and hopes like a passing dream
Are covered by shadows of night.

Come all ye dupes, ye millions of men
Who heeded my wishes like fools.
Take your share for aye of the galling chains
Under Him who in triumph rules.

You have lived and died for my noble cause;
Your souls are eternally marred.
You shall see no more than glimpses of light
Of Heaven, from which you are barred.

Then fling all your hopes, my friends, to the winds
As echoes of sadness reply.
You will feel henceforth the deeper degrees
Of the hell which beneath us lies.

Take heed all ye peoples and think it not odd
Ever barred from fellowship sweet.
All Heaven is witness ere the Son of God
Offered freedom at Calvary's defeat.

Too late to repent, too late I said;
Instead gnash your teeth with desire,
When the glorious Groom to the Bride is wed
As we slip into the lake of fire...

Anon

CONTACT THE AUTHOR

The author has used the contents of this book to establish a series of Bible study notes that can be very useful to home cells and other groups. If you would like to receive these Bible study notes, please send a USB STICK, together with a return addressed envelope to the following address:

J.A. Flanagan
P.O. Box 916,
Umtentweni
4235
KwaZulu Natal
South Africa

Additional copies of this book and other book
titles from DESTINY IMAGE EUROPE
are available at your local bookstore.

We are adding new titles every month!

To view our complete catalog online, visit us at:
www.eurodestinyimage.com

Send a request for a catalog to:

**Via Acquacorrente, 6
65123 - Pescara - ITALY
Tel. +39 085 4716623 - Fax +39 085 4716622**

"Changing the world, one book at a time."

Are you an author?

Do you have a "today" God-given message?

CONTACT US

We will be happy to review your manuscript
for a possible publishing:

publisher@eurodestinyimage.com